WAGNER'S OPERAS

RICHARD WAGNER

From a photograph taken in May, 1877, in London, where
Wagner had gone to conduct some concerts at the Albert Hall.
He was 64 years old. He had just completed the poem of
Parsifal. The year before, he had accomplished at the first
Bayreuth Festival the première of DER RING DES NIBELUNGEN.

Wagner's Operas

BY LAWRENCE GILMAN

MUSIC CRITIC OF
The New York Herald Tribune

FARRAR & RINEHART, INC.

NEW YORK · TORONTO

Contents

Author's Note

IN the title of this book, I have used the word "operas" in its loosely generic sense, for convenience of designation, to include *Tristan* as well as *Lohengrin*—although *Tristan,* in the specifically Wagnerian sense, is not an "opera," but a music-drama. After Wagner had conceived the plan of his *Ring* as a whole, he declared that he would "write no more operas." But he added, "as I do not wish to invent an arbitrary title for my [later] works, I call them 'dramas,' a term which will at least indicate clearly the standpoint from which the thing I offer should be accepted." Yet Wagner himself took a few private liberties in this matter. Although he characterizes *Tristan,* on the title-page of the score, as "Handlung in drei Aufzügen" ("Action in three Acts"), in his correspondence he does not mind alluding to it as "meine Oper, *Tristan*" (in a letter to B. Schotts Söhne, dated October 30, 1861, a year after the issue of the score).[1]

It is a pleasure to avow my obligation to the

---

[1] *Richard Wagners Briefe: Ausgewählt und erläutert von Wilhelm Altmann.* Bibliographisches Institut, Leipzig, 1925. Vol. II, p. 171. See also Vol. I, pp. 416, 418.

eminent musicologist, Dr. Otto Strobel, custodian of the Wagner archives at Wahnfried, Bayreuth, and the final authority on Wagnerian fact, for his courteous assistance in clearing up a number of points involved in my consideration of Wagner's works. The enhanced facility with which students of Wagner are now able to undertake the discussion of his creative methods is due chiefly to the invaluable research of Dr. Strobel in the great mass of new Wagnerian source-material which has been made accessible within recent years. Most of this became available after the death of Cosima Wagner in 1930, when the realistic wisdom of her son Siegfried and, later, of Siegfried's widow, Frau Winifred Wagner, the present *Herrin von Bayreuth,* allowed the disclosure of the Wahnfried archives, held inviolate by Cosima for almost half a century after Wagner's death. This material, of capital importance to students, critics, and historians, contains as its chief treasure a quantity of Wagner's manuscript sketches, memoranda, letters, diaries, and other musical and literary evidence bearing upon the inception and evolution of his works throughout his entire creative life. These inestimable documents, almost untraversable in mass and complexity, have been assembled and organized by Dr. Strobel with consummate skill; and the information which they contain, most of it hitherto unsuspected as well as unknown outside Wahn-fried, is gradually being placed by Dr. Strobel at the service of Wagnerian specialists.

There is apparently no end to the surprises contained in the new Wagnerian material that has emerged not only from Wahnfried, but from other sources, during the last decade or so. For example, the letters from Wagner to the Princess Marie Wittgenstein published in part by Richard Sternfeld in *Die Musik* in 1926-27 contained one of the most astonishing disclosures regarding the creative history of *Tristan und Isolde* which Wagnerian students have been vouchsafed. These eighteen letters are unincluded, so far as I am aware, in any of the numerous editions of Wagner's correspondence, and are still almost un-known to Wagnerian students outside Germany.

The new data concerning Wagner which are constantly issuing from various sources continue to invalidate many long-established assumptions regarding his procedures as an artist and the history of his works. It will probably never be easy to write with complete assurance of Wagner's life or art. The complexity of his character, the subtlety and profundity of his mind, the range of his activity and the vastness of his works will continue to make the task of the commentator peculiarly difficult and embarrassing—even should the necessary data be available.

AUTHOR'S NOTE

In common with all those who love and study Wagner, I am under an irreducible debt of gratitude to Ernest Newman (for me personally, an old and generous friend as well as an admired colleague). No one, I think, will henceforth be able to approach the formidable task of discussing Wagner without being better fitted for it by the example of uncompromising intellectual integrity, exhaustless scholarship, and piercing aesthetic intuition afforded by Newman in his contributions to our knowledge and appreciation of Wagner, now (as I write) approaching their culmination in the magistral Life in course of completion and publication—an unrivalled work, achieved with unflagging mastery, plenary devotion, and beautiful imaginative truth.

For permission to quote, by special arrangement, a number of excerpts from Cosima Wagner's long-unknown diary of her life with Wagner, and from her letters, my thanks are due to Alfred A. Knopf, Inc., authorized publishers of Richard Count Du Moulin-Eckart's *Cosima Wagner,* translated from the German by Catherine Alison Phillips (New York and London, 1930).

I am privileged likewise to quote, by special permission, several passages from the *Letters of Richard Wagner to Anton Pusinelli,* translated and edited by Elbert Lenrow; published by Alfred A. Knopf, Inc., New York, 1932.

x

AUTHOR'S NOTE

I have quoted from the collection of *Wagner's Letters,* selected and edited by Wilhelm Altmann, published in Germany by the Bibliographisches Institut, Leipzig (1925), and in England and America by J. M. Dent & Sons, Ltd., and E. P. Dutton & Co. (1927); from the *Letters of Richard Wagner to Mathilde Wesendonck,* translated and prefaced by William Ashton Ellis (London, H. Grevel & Co., 1905); from Ellis's English version of Wagner's Prose Works (London, Kegan Paul, Trench, Trübner & Co., Ltd., 1907); and from Wagner's *Mein Leben* (*My Life*), published in America by Dodd, Mead & Co., New York, 1911.

I am indebted to various colleagues and friends for assistance in the preparation of these chapters. Those unfailingly wise, gracious, long-suffering, and helpful guardians of the New York Public Library's invaluable "Music Library" in East 58th Street—Miss Dorothy Lawton, Miss Gladys Chamberlain, and Miss Mary Lee Daniels —have endured my importunities with angelic patience and friendliness, and have supplied my needs when my own library did not yield the required material.

Both Mr. Elbert Lenrow, the distinguished American musicologist, and my accomplished colleague of the *Herald Tribune's* music staff,

Mr. Jerome D. Bohm, have given me indispensable assistance in reading proof.

Miss Gertrude Wolf, my friend of many years, has borne without complaint the task of deciphering my villainous manuscript, and her help has been invaluable. Miss Eleanor Shane, of the Littleton, New Hampshire, Public Library, has been weariless in the irksome task of preparing the typescript for the press; and Mrs. Helen Herbert, of Sugar Hill, New Hampshire, has hastened the completion of my work by her kind coöperation and efficiency.

I have only to add that the following chapters undoubtedly contain a variety of things which should have been said differently, or not at all. Like most of those temerarious beings who set down words and publish them, I am aware of my inescapable subjection to the innate and incurable viciousness of the subconscious mind, which goes its own way, regardless of its victim's purposes and wishes—treacherous, vindictive, and corrupt. And doubtless I have committed errors unchargeable to the subconscious mind. Inevitably, sooner or later, I shall find myself recalling those sorrowful words of Dr. Johnson's Preface to his Dictionary in which he asks the reader to consider that "sudden fits of inadvertency will surprise vigilance, slight avocations will seduce attention, and casual eclipses of the mind will darken learning."

TO MY DAUGHTER

Preface

By Way of Dedication

Dear B——:

You may remember that after you had graciously accepted the dedication of this book you asked me what kind of book it was to be; and that I tried, rather sketchily, to tell you. I should like to make another and more deliberate attempt to answer your question.

It may be well to say at the outset what this book is not. It is not a guide to Wagner's operas. It does not tell their stories, nor, as a rule, their histories. It does not describe their legendary backgrounds, nor lead the student or prospective hearer methodically and informingly through their scores. There are countless books that do these things, and do them admirably. Nor have I attempted to deal, save incidentally, with Wagner the human being.

You may now, I think, begin to realize the various things this book is not, and perhaps the thing which actually it is, or aims to be.

It is a sheaf of notes or studies addressed to those who care deeply for Wagner's music.

It is a book chiefly about the greatness of Wagner the musician; and the author takes leave to discover the presence and the measure of that greatness wherever he quite willfully sees fit —in certain portions of certain earlier works; overwhelmingly in the operas after 1853. I am concerned with Wagner only as an artist, and chiefly as an artist in his maturer phases. I might have used, as a text for this book, two sentences that Newman wrote not many years ago: "The more I know my Wagner, the more convinced I am that this is the most wonderful artist-mind that the world has ever seen." . . . "From liking of Wagner as a musician, I have gone to adoration." Though for me that latter declaration is a little on the cautious side: for I began, not with liking, but with adoration of the artist who had written *Tristan*. That was in the distant days when I was very young, and used to smuggle the orchestral score to bed with me and try to read it when I was supposed to be asleep. Today, after nearly two hundred hearings of *Tristan,* and almost as many of Wagner's other major works, I am still wordless before this unbelievable music that I have dared to write about. Liszt called Wagner "den Unglaublichen" ("the incredible one"). That he was, and is.

It is possible that a shared experience is not entirely futile. One of the more plausible excuses for writing about music at all is the chance, the hope at least, that, if all goes well, the writer may be able to communicate something of his own conviction that great music brings new worlds about us. A tolerant word or two might be ventured for the usefulness of that type of commentator who, as one of them has said, "takes his place among us to stimulate our attention when it falters, and perhaps to supplement our responsiveness out of his own store of observation and reflection. . . . His position is not to command, but to quicken: to be less the schoolmaster than the fellow-student." I find it heartening to remember the definition proposed by Mr. Santayana for what he indulgently called "the art and function of criticism": "a reasoned appreciation of human works by a mind not wholly ignorant of their subject or occasion"; and I suspect that one of the exercises of that function may be the recognition and extolling of a sovereign art. Like the ideal artist, the ideal critic (if there be any such monocerous creature) should be filled with a never-ending awareness of the prime and mysterious function of the greatest music: that function by virtue of which it offers us a means of entering into the extended self of the imagination, so that we become, for a while, one with the creative musician, as he himself has become

Everyman. A master of music said: "Thus I can speak to my brothers."

Experiences such as these are infinitely to be treasured. The memories that they leave with us give existence a new validity and richness. They become part of those deep and secure and restorative possessions of the spirit which transcend the years.

❧ ❧ ❧

You will notice that in the course of these chapters I have set down my impressions of certain exceptional interpreters of Wagner's music whose re-creations of that music in our time, on the stage or in the orchestra pit, are indissolubly bound up with the work of art itself. For artists of the type I have in mind are able, by means of some baffling process of the imagination and the will, to disengage essentials. Inexplicably, magically, they realize for us Isolde's dedicated passion, Brünnhilde's cosmic grief, Elisabeth's clairvoyant and heroic innocence: through them the mystery is accomplished, and we perceive that devoutness and spiritual integrity and genius have fulfilled their appointed tasks.

It was said by a critic of experience and sensibility that the art of a certain unexcelled interpreter in the theatre was "to do over again the sculpture of the soul upon the body." Those of us who are living through a memorable period in the lyric theatre of America know what this can mean. We may have heard a singer of our own renascent day who is able to fill Isolde's "Lass mich sterben!" with a sense of consecration so exalting that the tragedy's far-off, predestined evening begins to fall about us as we listen, and we hear the distant, lifting pinions of the Liebestod.

Thus I account it one of the major obligations of the critic who lives in a time of great interpreters to keep alive within himself, and to communicate if he is able, the sense of that greatness. For greatness of this sort is tragically fugitive. It sets its mark upon the history of the re-creative mind in some favored decade or generation, and then is gone forever, save as it endures in the memories of those survivors who have been privileged to receive its impact and its stamp.

L. G.

Sugar Hill,
New Hampshire,
May 13, 1937.

WAGNER'S OPERAS

I

Wagner and the Present Day

ONE FEBRUARY day in 1883 the wife and children of Richard Wagner, seated at lunch in their palazzo at Venice, were startled by the violent ringing of the bell from Wagner's room, and the entrance of a white-faced servant with a message to Cosima from her husband bidding her come at once and to send a gondolier for the doctor. By half past three that afternoon the extraordinary genius who had been, in his indomitable art, "avid of all dominion and all mightiness, all sorrow, all delight, all topless grandeurs, all beauty, and all starry majesties," became

> . . . successive unto nothing
> But patrimony of a little mould,
> And entail of four planks . . .

Many things have happened in the world of music since that receding day. We have come to know and cherish the later Brahms, Strauss, Debussy, Sibelius; we have encountered Schönberg and Stravinsky and Bartok, Berg and Krenek, Hindemith and Antheil and Varèse; have em-

3

bosomed and dislodged the sadly shrunken "Six";
have submitted ourselves to the tonal ideology of
Dmitri Szostakowicz and his symphonic gospel
of proletarian faith. Above all, we have learned
that the art of music is a living organism; that
none of its principles is immutable; that the symphonies of Sibelius, and Debussy's *Pelléas,* and
Strauss' *Elektra,* and Schönberg's *Pierrot Lu-
naire,* and Stravinsky's *Sacre,* and Berg's *Woz-
zeck,* are no less autonomous and valid because
they stand in the gigantic shadow of *Tristan* and
the *Ring.*

Yet Wagner prevails increasingly: prevails
with a vitality that is astonishing even to those
who have the completest faith in his genius and
his immortality. In most countries, and especially
in America, his operas exert today a power of
attraction unequalled by those of any other writer
for the lyric stage. The Wagner Cycles that are
given every Winter in New York crowd the
Metropolitan, and are heard by audiences who
listen with that absorption which Wagner's
music seems always to compel. These Wagner
Cycles, given outside the regular subscription,
attract a public not only of exceptional cultiva-
tion, seriousness, and zest, but one peculiarly
single-minded—one that comes to hear great
music of a certain kind, and for no other reason,

4

devoting itself with concentration to the work of genius that is being set before it.

It is noteworthy that Wagner—in a letter written to the Philharmonic Society of New York on April 4, 1873 (he was then in his sixtieth year, and was about to begin the scoring of *Götterdäm-merung*)—should have expressed himself with touching confidence regarding his audiences in America. "I look upon it," he wrote, "as a reward of my efforts in behalf of art that I have won friends in the new and (for me, unfortunately) strange world whose sympathy has reared for me a sort of spiritual home." As late as 1879, three years after the Bayreuth première of the *Ring,* he could still say, in one of the engrossing series of letters written to King Ludwig II of Bavaria which have recently been given to the world through the enlightened public spirit of Frau Winifred Wagner, that "the Anglo-American race" more and more aroused his interest. "These people," he declared, "are serious, and take things seriously. . . . I often look toward America when I despair of seeing my work really taking root . . ."

Long ago his work took root in this "strange world" of which he spoke—a world which has become increasingly a spiritual home for his art.

The Wagner audiences at the Metropolitan draw today upon a new and eager public, young, unjaded, inquisitive, and alert, whose development must be attributed in large part to the activities of the Opera Guild, that organization of music lovers which owes its formation and influence to the imaginative vision and the practical sagacity of Mrs. August Belmont.

Not long ago it was being said that in America the intelligent young cared nothing for opera—that it did not exist for them, except as an enforced and penitential bore. That statement is apparently subject to correction. It would seem that many of the intelligent young have learned to care at least for Wagner, as though they had made their own discerning choice between those two worlds comprised within the theatre: the world existing primarily for our diversion, and that other world which offers us not diversion, but experience—an experience standing apart from ordinary existence, lifting us into those great moods of the spirit that alter profoundly the depth and range of our perceptions and the texture of our lives.

❦ ❦ ❦

Yet probably there are many, certainly there are some, who ask themselves, "What have we, with our music of today that is congenially unbemused and laconic, austere and astringent, hard and lean and bare: music that expresses us,

6

that is our own—what have we to do with this other music of an irrecoverable past? What is our concern with Wagner and his erring gods and sacrificial heroines, his gossiping forest birds that fly by wire, his papier-mâché dragons, his lovers who love and forget and love again (as it may seem to the observation of the casual) by virtue of drugs from some magical and epic pharmacy? What does Wagner mean to us?"

Well, what *does* Wagner mean to us today? In what relation do we stand to him? What does Wagner the artist yield to that Posterity which may, for our present purposes, be identified with ourselves? What does he reveal, not merely to the ear and eye and mind of faith, but to the resolute and dispassionate scrutiny of aesthetic appraisal, in the second half-century of his presumable immortality?

The first result of such dispassionate scrutiny, I think, is the conviction that this musical dramatist, as he thought himself, is primarily a musician; the second is, that this musician remains prodigious.

Probably the most important fact that has been yielded by the enlightened Wagnerian scholarship of recent years is the conclusion, sustained by irrefutable evidence, that Wagner derived his dramas from his music rather than his music from his dramas: that he was a dramatic symphonist who thought musically, rather than a musical dramatist who thought dramatically.

He himself was in large degree responsible for the long-accepted tradition that viewed him as a dramatic poet employing music as merely one of the means whereby the drama was to be expressed and realized—as a handmaiden, cherished and marvellously efficient, to be sure, but still a handmaiden. "With regard to all my dramatic works" (after *The Flying Dutchman*), he wrote in *A Communication to My Friends* (1851), "I was in the first instance poet, and only in the complete working-out of the poem did I become once more musician." [1] The fact that the situation was precisely the reverse—that in the first instance he was the musician, and that only later did he become the dramatic poet— seems to have been recognized by Wagner himself only in part and only occasionally. Goethe said of one of his own works that it contained more than he himself knew; and something of the same sort might be said concerning Wagner's attitude toward his creations. He spent an immense amount of time and energy in asserting the primacy in himself of the dramatist and poet, and the junior partnership of the musician; and

[1] He was discerning enough to add, however: "I was a poet conscious in advance of the power of musical expression for the working-out of my poems."

it is scarcely strange that for many years the world took him at his word, seeing that relationship and the works produced by it as Wagner himself insisted that they be seen.

Yet as early as January, 1844, when he was working on the composition of *Tannhäuser,* he wrote from Dresden to his young friend and admirer Karl Gaillard a letter in which he set forth what now appears to have been a remarkably objective and faithful description of his actual procedure in evolving his works. "In the first place," he explained to Gaillard, "I am attracted only to subjects the poetic and musical significance of which strike me simultaneously. Before I go on to write a verse or plot or scene, I am already intoxicated by the musical aroma of my subject. I have every note, every characteristic motive in my head, so that when the versification is complete and the scenes arranged, the opera is practically finished for me; the detailed musical treatment is just a peaceful meditative after-labor, the real moment of creation having long preceded it."

Wagner might have written those words at any time between the composition of *The Flying Dutchman* and the completion of *Parsifal*—if he had chosen to discard that contradictory thesis which he was so persistent in stating: for, as Ernest Newman remarked in his *Wagner as*

9

Man and Artist, the fact "that the musician in Wagner ruled the poet is plain enough to us now, but it was always denied by Wagner himself." It was denied by him except when the truth broke through his curious shell of self-delusion; and then he could have echoed Nietzsche's profound assertion, in *The Birth of Tragedy,* that "music is the essential idea of the world; drama is but the reflection of this idea, a detached adumbration of it." He could have echoed, too, that other saying of Nietzsche's on which he meditated while he was completing *Götterdämmerung* at Bayreuth: "As the child in the womb is nourished by its mother's blood, so drama draws its life from music. This is a mystery."

In Wagner's case, the original creative kindling appears always to have been musical. Afterward he found a poetic and dramatic vessel for the flame.

As he himself informed Gaillard, the musical conception of his subjects habitually preceded their dramatic and poetic realization. But sometimes this inversion of the customary formula was even more pronounced, and musical ideas related to a conception with which he was not actively concerned at all would intrude themselves while he was working out a wholly different subject.

An example of this process is recorded in a

letter (unknown until a decade or so ago) from Wagner to the young Princess Marie Wittgenstein, daughter of Liszt's disagreeable friend, the Princess Caroline Sayn-Wittgenstein. In Wagner's letter, written December 19, 1856, while he was at work on the composition of *Siegfried,* he says that he "wished today to compose further in *Siegfried,* but unexpectedly came to *Tristan*—for the present, music without words. But there are things for which I prefer to make music rather than verses. . . . Today, *Tristan* intruded with a melodic thread which wove itself anew every time I tried to get away from it, in such manner that I might have spun away at it all day."

Several things about this communication are worth noting. Wagner did not begin the dramatic text of *Tristan* until August, 1857, and he did not begin the composition-sketches of the music until October; yet here he is, eight months before the drama was written and ten months before the composition was begun, and with *Siegfried* as his major occupation, telling his correspondent that the *Tristan* music has begun to engross him, and that he could have "spun away at it all day"!

And how unblushingly Wagner the musician reveals himself in those slightly impatient references to the making of "verses"!

Writing again to the Princess Marie in the

following Spring (March 4, 1857),[2] Wagner remarks: "In the second Act of *Tristan*—but you know nothing about that yet. It is all, at present, only music": another curious statement, when we remember that the prose-sketch of the *Tristan* drama was still almost half a year ahead of him.

In May of the same year (1857), he wrote Mathilde Wesendonck that the Muse was "beginning to visit" him. "The first thing that came to me," he continued, "was a melody which at first I didn't in the least know how to place, until all at once the words for it came to me from the last scene of *Siegfried*"—the composition of which he did not take up until a dozen years later, at Triebschen.

The buoyant melody that forms the subject of the fugato at the end of the love duet of *Siegfried*—it accompanies Siegfried's words:

> "Sie ist mir ewig,
> ist mir immer,
> Erb' und Eigen,
> Ein und All' "—

occurred to Wagner, according to his own statement, during the composition of *Tristan und Isolde,* while he was seeking the joyful melody

---

[2] Dr. Wilhelm Altmann, one of the editors of Wagner's correspondence, maintains that the date sometimes assigned to this letter—January, 1857—is incorrect.

of the Shepherd that announces the sighting of Isolde's ship.[3]

The great World's Heritage motive, first heard in the latter part of the scene between Erda and the Wanderer in Act III of *Siegfried,* was composed for *Die Sieger,* the Buddhistic drama sketched by Wagner in 1856, but abandoned—though certain of its elements were incorporated into *Tristan* and *Parsifal.*

And who would have supposed, before the publication in 1929 of extracts from Cosima Wagner's diary, that some of the most important thematic material in the last Act of *Siegfried* was originally intended by Wagner for use as chamber music?

It is certainly an astonishing and revealing fact, indicative of the fundamentally musical character of Wagner's mind, that when he composed at Triebschen in 1869 the music for Brünnhilde's speech in her scene with Siegfried beginning, "Ewig war ich, ewig bin ich," he employed for this purpose two themes conceived for use in a string quartet that he had wanted to write at Starnberg almost five years before. The first of these, known to the nominators of Wagner's leading-motives as the *Friedensmelodie,* is the serenely lovely subject which Wagner also used

[3] See Wagner's letter to Mathilde Wesendonck from Lucerne, July 9, 1859.

as the chief theme of the *Siegfried Idyll*—that exquisite symphonic aubade composed in November, 1870, as a birthday greeting for Cosima and in honor of their young son Siegfried. The second of the two themes which came into existence as material for chamber music is that known to the commentators as the World's Treasure motive. It is heard in the music-drama at Brünnhilde's words, "O Siegfried, Herrlicher! Hort der Welt!"; and ke its companion, it is used also in the *ted Idyll.*

ently there was in Wagner's mind some deep-seated and profoundly right identification between the imaginative impulse which had impelled the creation of the two string-quartet themes conceived in 1864, when Cosima, foreseeing all and risking all, had given herself unreservedly to him at Starnberg, and that later impulse which caused him to find in those themes the fitting expression for Brünnhilde's "Ewig war ich" speech in *Siegfried* five years later. He must have felt that in the earlier music which had come into being at the time of his and Cosima's realization of their mutual need he had anticipated the music for Brünnhilde's conflict of emotions and intuitions in the final scene of *Siegfried* —her serene and lofty tenderness, her half-desperate, half-exultant acceptance of the destiny foreseen by her insight and her wisdom for Siegfried and herself and the divine and human worlds. We are told that Cosima regarded the use of the Starnberg themes in the love scene of *Siegfried* as "their true application."

It is obvious that we are finding here a process of musico-poetic generation far more subtle, instinctive, and inexplicable than the familiar procedure of setting a given dramatic text to music. All that is to enter into the structure and significance of the final composite art-work has already expressed itself, in essence, as music. And this music becomes finally something more than music. The drama, the poetry, the philosophy, the ideation, are caught up by the musician's imagination and transmuted into organized and fulfilling sound—achieve their ultimate expression, their exalting and unmistakable voice.

Thus it is Wagner the musician who emerges from the complex of aims and activities that involved him; it is Wagner the musician who towers across the years.

❋   ❋   ❋

Yet it may be doubted if there are many, even among musicians, who realize the magnitude of Wagner's achievement as a composer. Preposterous as it may appear to say so, Wagner's later scores are as yet imperfectly known; and it is still possible to stagger the average musician

15

by the assertion that Wagner, far from being, as he was long so innocently called, "formless," was the greatest master of tonal structure in the history of musical art.

"Greatness of dimension," said Burke, "is a powerful cause of the sublime." But in the typical scores of Wagner's maturity there is not only greatness of dimension, but a structural capacity of enormous range and resourcefulness. The art of music offers nothing to compare with the vastness and complexity of design and the gigantic power of organization that Wagner achieved in the music of *Der Ring des Nibelungen*. The sheer immensity of the thing is enough, in itself, to stop one's breath—this quadruple dramatic symphony that requires approximately fourteen hours to traverse; in which the web of music is cumulatively spun for as long as it would take to play a dozen symphonies the length of Beethoven's Ninth. Even the ablest of our contemporary musical minds would perhaps draw back in some dismay from the task of essaying a fourteen-hour composition achieved throughout with the closeness and continuity of texture and the formal logic of the polyphonic Bach and the symphonic Beethoven, and with a richness and variety of substance unequalled in any adventure that music has elsewhere undertaken.

The new musical scholarship that for a decade or so has been applying itself to an exhaustive technical study of Wagner's later works—the *Ring, Tristan, Die Meistersinger,* and *Parsifal* [4] —has demonstrated the fact that these imperfectly known scores are fundamentally symphonic in conception: that they are self-contained and self-sufficing organisms, tonal structures of prodigious amplitude and elaboration, planned with an architectural logic and symmetry yielding a significance quite apart from the music's aspect as an expression of the dramas to which it is related. It has been shown that these unexampled creations represent Wagner's application to his own art of the classic principles of contrast and balance and periodicity which are the basis of symphonic form.

Wagner, therefore, reveals himself to the mind of our day as an excelling master of musical structure, obeying an instinct for design that had its roots in the deep soil of the classicism that had nourished him, but which he developed, in his own way and for his own ends, upon a scale of unprecedented range and variety of implication.

The traditional view of him, a view that still

[4] The student is referred to the penetrating analyses of the musical structure of Wagner's later scores, presented with the elaborate detail and precision of mathematical demonstrations, in the epoch-making work of the German musicologist, Alfred Lorenz: *Das Geheimnis der Form bei Richard Wagner* (published at Munich, between 1924 and 1933, in four volumes, devoted respectively to the *Ring, Tristan, Meistersinger,* and *Parsifal*).

obtains to some extent among incurious musicians, regards him as a man of the theatre, a tonal dramatist who employed a formless music to do the playwright's will. We know now that this view is as remote from the fact as that equally naïve and unrealistic delusion which conceives of the essential Bach as an austere and undeviating formalist, a devotee of absolute music. It would be closer to the truth about Bach to say that he was essentially what his foremost expounder, the late Professor Terry, did not hesitate to call him—"an incorrigible romanticist." It would be closer to the truth about Wagner to say that he was essentially a classicist, one of the great logicians of musical art, distinguished by a toughness of cerebral fibre and an intellectual staying-power beside which the capacities of less audacious and powerful musical minds seem relatively limited. We are beginning to realize the surprising fact that Wagner, long regarded as the arch-corrupter who forcibly wedded the presumably virginal art of tones to the villain of the Drama, was actually a symphonist in his treatment of music as an expressional and delineative art; that his genius was primarily musical, and only secondarily dramatic. As between the art of Wagner and that of the Bach of the Passions, the Cantatas, and the Chorale-Preludes, it

18

might be said, with certain obvious reservations, that of the two, Wagner's mind was the more tough-fibred, classic, and abstract, and Bach's the more romantic, dramatizing, and concrete.

No matter how vivid the expressive implication, Wagner the musician was always in the ascendant. Though he himself was to some extent deluded on this point, as were many of his followers, we of today, who can look at his work in the proper perspective, seeing the wood despite the trees, have discovered that Wagner's Immortal Beloved, unrecognized, unavowed, unconsciously adored, was the most aloof and proudest of the Muses, Euterpe—Euterpe in her divine, unchallenged purity, her sovereign dignity and pride.

Thus, slowly, the Wagner of legend, the Wagner of the received tradition, yields to the Wagner of untrammelled scrutiny and fresh report.

We confront in Wagner the paradox of a musician who, refusing to appear primarily as such before the world, triumphs finally through the greatness of his musicianship.

Some will continue to believe that as sheer music—as a fabric of organized and woven sound —Wagner's major scores are unapproached. "The greatness of an art is its intensity," said Keats;

and Wagner's music, when it faithfully bespeaks his genius, is the most intensely realized that we possess. ❧ ❧ ❧

But we must not allow ourselves to forget that this fabric of incandescent and engrossing sound is also the garment of a poet and a lord of souls, and that his music is a tongue of life. "The thing that amazes me," FitzGerald said of Shakespeare, "is that when I look into him, it is not a Book, but People living all about me." And it is to Shakespeare that we must go to find anything resembling the scope and richness and diversity of Wagner's multitudinous world, with its bewildering range of character and life, its width of human reference, its evocation of the wonder and might and mystery and enchantment of the Nature that bore us and enfolds us.

What a world it is, this world of Wagner's! What a pageant of humanity! The stirring of immemorial depths in the dark river, and the Temple of the Grail; Nibelheim, and Hunding's hut, and that Cornish garden "with high trees, on a clear summer night"; the tempests that gather among primeval hills, and the gray dusk of the Sagas; Siegfried's forest, and a cosmos in flames; the avarice of Alberich, and Hagen's hate; Sieglinde's tenderness, and Brünnhilde's lofty grief and divination, and the ripening of Sachs's spirit as he sits in the morning sunlight of his workroom, tranquil and assuaged, dreaming of old-world loveliness and old-world peace: these things become for us, in Wagner's music, timeless symbols of the natures and destinies of men and women and of the phases of the cradling earth.

This music, more frequently than any other, takes us into what a poet of today has simply and profoundly called "that great mood of infinity in which life is all spirit and passion." Wagner is the transfiguring poet par excellence because he lets us see his subjects, whether they be human or heroic fables or embodied passions or incarnate symbols of the high mysteriousness of human life and destiny—Hans Sachs or Senta or Wotan or Parsifal or Isolde—under the aspect of eternity, lifted into a universal greatness of implication, and charged with universal beauty and significance. For always there is the prophetic and subliminal Wagner, Wagner the mystic and the seer, whose music, for long, incredible moments, reminds us that we are greater than we knew.

II

The Early Operas and "The Flying Dutchman"

WAGNER'S first three operas belonged to his twenties. In none of them is the true Wagner more than vaguely and fleetingly foreshadowed, though in each of them there are intimations of what was to come. The music of his first completed opera,[1] *Die Feen* (*The Fairies*), was begun in 1832 or 1833, and finished in 1834, when he was twenty-one. It was never given in Wagner's lifetime. Its first performance took place five years after his death—at Munich, June 29, 1888; and during the next decade it had as many as seventy performances there.[2]

[1] Wagner's first attempt at an opera, which was to be a tragedy, *Die Hochzeit* (*The Wedding*), never got beyond a few fragments, composed and scored in 1832-33—an orchestral introduction, a chorus, and a septet. The fragments were published, in full score, in the *Gesamtausgabe* by Breitkopf and Härtel in 1912.

[2] *Die Feen* was revived in an elaborate production at the Württemberger Landestheater, Stuttgart, in the season of 1932-33, as part of a complete cycle of Wagner's stage-works given in commemoration of the fiftieth anniversary of his death; and on that occasion it was enthusiastically received. The Overture was performed in New York at concerts of the Philharmonic Society in 1915-16, and has since been repeated.

22

Wagner has left us his own account, in *A Communication to My Friends,* written in later years, of the composition of the ingenuous opus.

"On the model of one of Gozzi's fairy tales (*La Donna Serpente*)," he says, "I wrote for myself an opera text, in verse, *Die Feen.* The then predominant 'romantic' opera of Weber, and also of Marschner—who about this time made his first appearance on the scene, and that at my place of sojourn, Leipzig—determined me to follow in their footsteps. What I turned out for myself was nothing more than barely what I wanted, namely, an opera text. This I set to music, according to the impressions made upon me by Weber, Beethoven, and Marschner. However, what took my fancy in the tale of Gozzi was not merely its adaptability for an opera text, but the fascination of the subject itself: a fairy, who renounces immortality for the sake of a human lover, can become a mortal only through the fulfillment of certain difficult conditions, the non-compliance wherewith on the part of her earthly swain threatens her with the direst penalties. Her lover fails in the test, which consists in this: that however evil and repulsive she may appear to him (in an obligatory metamorphosis), he shall not reject her in his unbelief. In Gozzi's tale the fairy is now changed into a snake; the remorseful lover frees her from the spell by kissing the snake;

thus he wins her for his wife. I altered this denouement by changing the fairy into a stone and then releasing her from the spell by her lover's passionate song; while the lover—instead of being allowed to carry off the bride into his own country—is himself admitted by the fairy king to the immortal bliss of Fairyland, together with his fairy wife."

Wagner's lifelong preoccupation with the idea of redemption is indicated in *Die Feen;* and in the music there are foreshadowings of his subsequent works, half amusing, half startling— prophecies of the Wagner of *Tannhäuser, Lohengrin, Die Walküre,* even of the far-off *Tristan.* The music has charm and address. It is both juvenile and surprisingly mature, with flashes of arresting insight and impressive skill.

Wagner's second opera, *Das Liebesverbot* (*The Ban on Love*), was written between 1834 and 1836. Its subject, "transformed pretty freely," as Wagner puts it, was taken from Shakespeare's *Measure for Measure.* It was meant, he says, as a protest "against puritanical hypocrisy," and "tended boldly to exalt unrestrained sensuality." It was produced at Magdeburg, March 29, 1836, under Wagner's direction. Inadequately prepared, the result was a dismal fiasco. The music remained in manuscript for eighty-seven years after it was written. The vocal

24

and orchestral scores were published in 1922-23. In the latter year the opera was resurrected at Munich.

Wagner gave the score to King Ludwig II in 1866, proffering it, with a plea for indulgence, as a "youthful sin." For his patterns in composing the music he had turned from the German romantic composers to the more frivolous Italian and French opera of his time. His command of that style is sure and effective. The music is often delightful in its unpretentious and light-hearted way. It is astonishingly skillful; it has charm and wit and sprightliness and gusto. Some of its qualities are attributable to Wagner's models for the work—Donizetti and Auber, Bellini and Rossini. But that is of no great consequence, for Wagner puts something of his own unmistakable stamp upon them all. And we are not allowed to forget that a greater master is in the offing. Not only does the score include a theme that Wagner was afterward to use in *Tannhäuser* (the so-called Pardon motive), but the faint, far rumors of an unimaginable later music are audible at times in measures that sound like tentative experiments in the idiom of *Tristan,* and even of *Parsifal.*

Das Liebesverbot has been too summarily rejected by those who were impressed, not unnaturally, by Wagner's own disparagement of it.

The work calls for reëxamination. One would like to hear it tried out in America. After all, a novelty by Wagner would be an engaging experience—even if it were not another *Meistersinger.*

It is not *Das Liebesverbot* that is Wagner's "youthful sin," but *Rienzi,* the third of the three works of his young manhood that preceded *The Flying Dutchman* (it was begun at Riga in 1838 and completed at Paris in the Autumn of 1840, in Wagner's twenty-eighth year). Over this Brobdingnagian setting of Bulwer-Lytton's historical novel, the loyal Wagnerian is tempted to draw the veil of sorrowful silence. This all-too-faithful imitation of the Parisian "grand opera," this swollen, pretentious blend of banality and bombast, is a sore trial for lovers of the godlike Wagner of the greater works.

Wagner says in his *Communication to My Friends* that at the time of conceiving *Rienzi* he desired to satisfy "an eager longing to begin something on a grand and inspiring scale . . . This mood was fed and fostered by my reading Bulwer's *Rienzi.* From the misery of modern private life, whence I could nowhere glean the scantiest stuff for artistic treatment, I was borne away by the picture of a great historico-political event . . . In accordance with my particular artistic bent, however, I still kept more or less to the purely musical, or rather operatic standpoint. This Rienzi, with great thoughts in his head, great feelings in his heart, amid an entourage of coarseness and vulgarity, set all my nerves a-quivering with sympathy and love. Yet my plan for an art-work based thereon sprang first from the perception of a purely lyric element in the hero's atmosphere. The 'Messengers of Peace,' the Church's summons to awake, the Battle-Hymns—these were what impelled me to the opera *Rienzi*."

Writing in the same *Communication,* however, Wagner, with truly heroic candor and just a touch of inconsistency, says that in the preparation of this text he "took no thought for anything but the writing of an effective operatic libretto. The 'Grand Opera,' with all its scenic and musical display, its sensationalism and its massive vehemence, loomed large before me; and not merely to copy it, but, with reckless extravagance, to out-bid it in every detail, became the object of my artistic ambition. However," he adds, "I should be unjust to myself did I represent this ambition as my only motive for the conception and execution of my *Rienzi*. The subject really aroused my enthusiasm, and I put nothing into my sketch which had not a direct bearing on the grounds of this enthusiasm. My chief concern was Rienzi himself; and only when I felt quite contented with

27

him did I give rein to the idea of a 'grand opera.' Nevertheless, from a purely artistic point of view, this 'grand opera' was the pair of spectacles through which I unconsciously regarded my material . . . I always fixed my gaze upon the material itself, and did not keep my eye open for certain ready-made effects which I might wish to father on it by hook or crook; only, I saw it in no other light than that of a five-act opera, with five brilliant finales, and filled with hymns, processions, and the musical clash of arms."

It is not impossible that Wagner, when he penned this mixture of confession and attempted self-vindication, was troubled by a guilty conscience. However that may be, *Rienzi,* as it survives for us, scarcely justifies Wagner's assertion that he was inspired by the historic character who is its central figure. This operatic hero of Wagner's is far from the authentic Rienzi— Rienzi the visionary, the dreamer, the lover of "sacred Italy," the warrior and the man of peace. The downfall of Wagner's Rienzi is brought about externally and melodramatically, by the machinations of his enemies and the treachery and instability of his former friends. The real Rienzi came to a more tragic and ironic end. "We are betrayed," said Meredith, "by what is false within." And that was Rienzi's tragedy. His head was turned by his success. He abandoned his lofty

28

dreams, became gross and shifty and time-serving.

This human, tragical, and wholly credible figure was whitewashed and sentimentalized by that dubious young man, the Wagner of 1838-40. Rienzi is a lay figure in the opera, stuffed with sawdust and Meyerbeer, and tailored by Spontini. Studying this lamentable production, it is hard to avoid the conclusion that Wagner, despite his later attempts at self-justification, was deliberately trying, in his own words, to "outbid with reckless extravagance" the Parisian Grand Opera at its worst and most profitable. The poverty-stricken composer had his eye on Paris, that potential operatic gold-mine for all those who could qualify (had not Meyerbeer banked 300,000 francs by *Les Huguenots?*). In *Rienzi* we have the marketable thing in its perfection, with its clamor and glare and fustian, its orgy of choruses, grand marches, grand airs, duos, trios, ballets, heaven-storming finales; its blaring, incontinent trumpets; its festal processions and ecclesiastical pomp.[3]

And this was all, in the outcome, that the tragedy of Rienzi apparently meant to Wagner.

[3] But though *Rienzi* had been intended for Paris, Wagner came to realize that there was no immediate hope of its production there. "I decided," he wrote, "to complete it in German with a view to a German theatre, and I selected Dresden." *Rienzi* was given at Dresden, with enormous success, on October 20, 1842.

There is no denying the crude vigor of the music; and it has something of that quality which Wagner always possessed, the quality of salient invention. The musical ideas that he was willing to put on paper in his early manhood were often harrowing; but one remembers them. Take, for example, the Prayer theme from *Rienzi*. It is not a theme that even the most indulgent would call distinguished; yet it sticks in the mind; one wishes it would not.

Yes, *Rienzi* is the cardinal Wagnerian sin. So let us forgive and forget it, if we can, and pass on to the first of his representative operas, *The Flying Dutchman,* the drama of which he sketched (it is hard to believe) while he was still occupied with *Rienzi.*

❦　　❦　　❦

It was Sainte-Beuve's belief that there is in every man a poet who dies young. It is equally true that there is in every poet a man who dies young. If one wants an example, consider the case of Wagner. It is clear that the predominantly crass and external Wagner of 1840, the Wagner of *Rienzi,* had almost entirely died out of the Wagner who composed the music of *The Flying Dutchman* in 1841.[4]

[4] Even while Wagner was still at work on *Rienzi,* he completed, in January, 1840, the first version of his noble and

He was scarcely exaggerating when he wrote, toward the end of his days: "So far as my knowledge goes, I can find in the life of no artist so striking a transformation, in so short a time, as is evident between *Rienzi* and *The Flying Dutchman,* the former of which was scarcely finished when the latter was almost ready." After the empty, pretentious *Rienzi,* with its strut and blare and its monstrous dimensions, the elevated fervor and sincerity and concentration of *The Flying Dutchman* announce a work that seems to have issued from another mind and time and period. Despite its conventionalities, its incongruities of style and substance, its retention of many of the traditional operatic formulas, *The Flying Dutchman* is nevertheless, in its flawed, inchoate way, a great work, great in spiritual substance, in loftiness of mood, and in much of its actual dramatic and musical texture. It is the first of Wagner's true music-dramas: here the musician and the dramatic poet interact, each kindling each. "From here," says Wagner in his *Communication,* "begins my career as poet, and my farewell to the mere concocter of opera texts. And yet I took no sudden leap. In no wise was I influenced by reflection . . . My course was new. It was bidden me by my inner mood, and forced

prophetic *Faust Overture,* which Dannreuther justly called "the first work that has the true stamp of Wagner."

31

upon me by the pressing need to impart this mood to others."

Wagner composed the music of *The Flying Dutchman* at Meudon and in Paris in a time of poverty and wretchedness so dire that he thought of suicide. The score was completed in the Autumn of 1841.[5]

❧ ❧ ❧

Of those works which are at all representative of his genius, *The Flying Dutchman* was least familiar to the present generation of American opera-goers, especially in New York, before it was revived at the Metropolitan in the season of 1930-31, after an absence of twenty-two years from the repertoire. The itinerant "Wagner Opera Company" had performed it several times at the Manhattan Opera House in 1923 and 1924; but with those exceptions, the woes of Wagner's accursed and mysterious wanderer had been withheld from observation in most American opera houses for almost a quarter of a century. Yet even today, after the Metropolitan revivals of 1930 and 1937—in the latter of which the role of Senta was assumed by Kirsten Flagstad—*The Flying Dutchman* has none too many friends.

[5] I am informed by Dr. Otto Strobel, custodian of the Wagner archives at Bayreuth, that the manuscript orchestral score of *The Flying Dutchman* (in its original form) bears the conclusion-date: "Meudon bei Paris 21 Octob. 18. Richard Wagner."

"THE FLYING DUTCHMAN"

If anyone could have established this youthful work of Wagner's in the affections of most American Wagner lovers it is the remarkable Norwegian singing-actress whose advent made so memorable that season at the Metropolitan which linked the end of Mr. Gatti-Casazza's consulship with the beginning of Mr. Edward Johnson's. Mme. Flagstad, who had made her American debut at the Metropolitan as Sieglinde in *Die Walküre* on Saturday afternoon, February 2, 1935, appeared as Senta, for the first time anywhere, on January 7, 1937. By the time she had sung the role four times she seemed to have made it not only a natural extension of her artistic personality, but an embodiment of the naïve and ecstatic dreamer of Wagner's dramatic fable, the selfless, sacrificial woman of the mariner's anguished hope.

The blend of poise and sensibility, vibrancy and resolution, strength and tenderness, pity and heroic faith, that makes this embodiment so rare, is conveyed to us by Mme. Flagstad from the first moment that we see her, sitting entranced, brooding, surrounded by the spinning maidens, but immeasurably apart from them. We hear it in every tone of her voice as she sings the ballad that Wagner called "the picture *in petto* of the entire drama." We hear it when Senta joins her voice with the Dutchman's in the rapturous duet.

Cosima Wagner once described to Richard a certain portrait that had impressed her deeply as "an apotheosis of simplicity." There could be no apter phrase for Flagstad's Senta. Wagner insisted upon Senta's fundamental naïveté. But this variety of naïveté is complex and profound—the naïveté that is characteristic of great natures. In his article on the proper performance of *The Flying Dutchman,* Wagner remarks that "only in the heart of an utterly naïve girl, a girl of the Norwegian North, could such an exalted monomania as Senta's take possession."

Unpleasant persons have said that Wagner's Senta was "hysterical." They are the same sort of persons who have said that Joan of Arc was hysterical. But hysteria may be an expression of the valorous and selfless, as well as of the feeble and self-indulgent. Wagner himself, with one of his fine strokes of irony, calls Senta "morbid," enclosing the word within quotation marks. Possibly Senta would have been a poor hand at golf or squash or tennis. Yet it is not difficult to think of her plunging with zest, on sunny, windy days, into the "salt, unplumbed, estranging sea" that washed the rocky coast near Daland's home—that sea into which in fact she leaped, with tragic fortitude and epic faith, at the end of Wagner's dramatic parable of sacrificial and heroic love.

❀   ❀   ❀

One may doubt whether the qualities of *The Flying Dutchman* have as yet been fairly assessed by most admirers of Wagner's genius. The work is usually regarded somewhat cavalierly as a product of Wagner's immaturity—which, to be sure, it is. Yet the word "immaturity" is one to be used with caution in discussing any product of a mind that is affected with creative genius. There are pages in *The Flying Dutchman* that are not to be forgotten: pages extraordinary for their power and mastery, and for their exhibition of an outstanding trait of Wagner's imagination—the power of vivid and seizing characterization.

In this opera of Wagner's fiery young manhood we find what we so often find in the early Wagner and so seldom in the later Wagner—a disconcerting blend of greatness and inferiority. Ideas of superb power and distinction are jostled by others patterned according to the clichés and conventions of their period. There are few thematic ideas in all Wagner more pregnant and forcible, more unmistakably the product of a creative imagination of the first rank, than the chief theme of the score, that which begins the Overture—the motive of the Dutchman himself, the doomed wanderer. That bleak and inexorable phrase for the brass, under the "empty fifth" sustained by the strings and woodwind, belongs in the class of those triumphantly expressive themes, charged with intense and concentrated power, whereby Wagner attests his claim to be ranked as the most articulate of composers. Only a musical imagination of the first order could have conceived it.

Who but Wagner could have made us feel the mystery and terror of the Dutchman's ghostly ship so surely and instantly as he has done with those three terrific F's that we hear from the timpani and tuba and string basses in the first scene as Vanderdecken's ship, looming through the storm with her black masts and blood-red sails, casts anchor with a thunderous crash? How felicitous, too, is the young master's treatment of that moment of tense and fateful silence in the Second Act when the dream-haunted maiden and the Dutchman first gaze, spellbound, on each other, with only the soft mutter of the timpani breaking the suspensive silence! And in all the range of music-drama is there anything more simply and more completely achieved than that grisly pianissimo chord of C-sharp minor for the horns and bassoon which, in the first scene of the Third Act, answers the cheerful C major call of the Norwegian maidens, with their baskets of food and wine, as they hail the spectral, sinister, darkened ship where it lies at its moorings wrapped in deathlike silence?

In such things as these are unmistakable

prophecies of the great dramatic imagination that was afterward to give us the *Ring* and *Tristan*.

On the other hand, the Perfect Wagnerite will find himself uneasy over certain pages in *The Flying Dutchman*. Admirable as are the finest things in the work, they are qualified by numerous examples of the early Wagner's defective faculty of self-examination. An English critic wrote concerning the Senta (or Redemption) theme that "it pictures not a heroine who will sacrifice herself for an idea, but a Hausfrau who will always have her husband's supper ready and his slippers laid to warm on the stove shelf." Perhaps that is going a little far. Nevertheless, the Senta theme is scarcely a distinguished one. Wagner puts it to eloquent use, especially at the close of the Overture and of the opera. But Wagner's Senta is greater than the theme that he contrived for her.

Wagner gives us some even less costly things in *The Flying Dutchman* score—of which the least to be treasured, perhaps, is Erik's F major Cavatina in Act III. Wagner's conscience may have troubled him a bit when he thought of this number; for ten years after he had composed it, he wrote, in his *Remarks on Performing "The Flying Dutchman,"* that "the tenor who should give a sugary rendering to the 'Cavatina' would do me a sorry service, for it ought instead to breathe distress and heartache"—which is a good deal like urging your breakfast companion not to sweeten the strawberry jam.

❧   ❧   ❧

The score of *The Flying Dutchman,* in its present form, is to some extent a hybrid, a curious and instructive mixture of musical styles.

The opera was completed originally in 1841, when Wagner was twenty-eight; but certain passages in the score as we now possess it are the issue of revisions made by the incomparably greater Wagner of the *Tristan* period. In 1860, the year after he completed *Tristan,* Wagner revised and partly recomposed the last fifty-three measures of the Overture, transforming the coda into a peroration of exalted and luminous beauty.

This particular revision of the score is the one alluded to by Wagner in letters to Mathilde Wesendonck from Paris in the Spring of 1860: "I have made a new close for the Overture of *The Flying Dutchman,* which pleases me much, and also made an impression on the audience at my concert . . . Now that I have written Isolde's last transfiguration [*letzte Verklärung*], at last I could find alike the right close for *The Flying Dutchman* Overture." [6]

[6] The manuscript score of this final version of the Overture is dated by Wagner: "RW Paris. 19 Jan. 60." Dr. Strobel conjectures that the melodic form of the last ten measures may date from a revision made by Wagner in 1852; but the instrumentation

"THE FLYING DUTCHMAN"

One of the most haunting passages in Wagner's letters is that in which he told his publisher, Schott, in December, 1869,—when he had completed all his operas except *Siegfried* (the last Act), *Götterdämmerung,* and *Parsifal,*—that he would like, as he expressed it, "to replenish *The Flying Dutchman* with improvements, and then devote my remaining years, at my convenience, to a gradual revision of my other works." A rewritten *Flying Dutchman,* to say nothing of a rewritten *Lohengrin* and *Tannhäuser,* benefiting throughout from the enhanced imaginative power and the ripened art that Wagner's maturity could have brought to it, would have been a wonderful thing indeed. Alas, he never found the opportunity for that task. Yet the music of *The Flying Dutchman,* as we have it, is indispensable. In it we confront, for the first time, the Wagner who abides.

of these measures, and the composition of the twenty-one measures that begin with the first entrance of the harp in the coda, date from 1860.

III

"Tannhäuser"

IT WOULD be interesting to know how many opera-goers realize that when they attend a performance of *Tannhäuser* at the Metropolitan, and arrive early enough, they will hear more than half an Act that is for the most part not *Tannhäuser* at all, but a sort of appendix to the score of *Tristan und Isolde,* blent with prophecies of *Götterdämmerung* and *Parsifal.* There will be moments, indeed, when they may find themselves wondering if the Venus of the long, candescent, tragical duet with Tannhäuser is not a sort of premonitory Kundry who has wandered backward in time from Klingsor's Magic Garden into the superheated caverns of the Hörselberg.

How many Wagnerians could put their hands on their hearts and swear that they realize just what Wagner did for them when he returned to the immature *Tannhäuser* of his Dresden years, after a decade and a half of unparalleled artistic growth, and recomposed an essential portion of his early score with the subtlety and power of his ripened art, at a time when his veins were still throbbing with the ichor of *Tristan und Isolde?*

A good many music lovers are perhaps insufficiently alert to the fact that *Tannhäuser* is actually a duplex score: not one work, but two. One of these works, as students of operatic history are aware, is the Dresden version of 1845, composed by Wagner in his early and still clumsy thirties.[1] The other is the Paris version of 1860-61, embodying those revisions and additions composed with the sorcerous and fine-fingered mastery of his middle age, soon after he had finished *Tristan.*

In the period that intervened between the old *Tannhäuser* and the partly new, Wagner had developed from a fumbling genius into a sovereign of art, and he had completed three epochal masterworks and part of a fourth. The Bacchanale and the Venusberg duet in the Paris version of *Tannhäuser* are the issue of the powerful brain and inexhaustible imagination that had already yielded not only *Tristan und Isolde,* but *Rheingold, Die Walküre,* and two-thirds of *Sieg-*

---

[1] Wagner began the music of *Tannhäuser* at Dresden in the Summer of 1843, in his thirty-first year, and finished the score in the Spring of 1845. The first performance was at Dresden, October 19, 1845. Wagner changed the denouement, and the opera was given at Dresden with its new ending on August 1, 1847. The extensive revisions for the Paris production were composed in 1860-61, in Wagner's forty-eighth year; and this transforming version of the work was performed at the Paris Opéra, March 13, 18, and 24, 1861.

fried, and that held the seeds of *Die Meister-singer, Götterdämmerung,* and *Parsifal.*

What had happened, it may be recalled, was that fifteen years after the Dresden première of *Tannhäuser,* Wagner was invited to prepare his early opera for a Paris production commanded by Napoleon III, who had been requested by the Princess Metternich, as a personal favor, to have *Tannhäuser* mounted at the Opéra. Wagner proceeded to revise the first two scenes of his score: the Bacchanalian revels at the court of Venus within a grotto of the Hörselberg, and the following duet between Venus and Tannhäuser. He undertook these revisions partly as a modified concession to the taste of an influential portion of the Parisian public of those days, which demanded a maximum of seductive choreography and a minimum of music-drama, and partly to satisfy his own insatiable demand for artistic perfection. He shortened the original Overture, omitting the coda, and making the Overture lead without pause into the Bacchanale. He did not otherwise change the Overture: but he altered extensively the Bacchanale, which he transformed from the tame and pallid divertissement of the Dresden version into a gigantic and terrifying blaze of sensual frenzy, written with a searing intensity that makes even the music of *Tristan* sound temperate; and he rewrote and expanded the scene between Venus and Tannhäuser which follows it, enhancing immeasurably its beauty and expressiveness.

The result of this labor got him nowhere, in a material sense. He had refused to provide a ballet in the Second Act, and that was his undoing: for the most consequential subscribers dined late, and what occurred in the First Act did not count, since they were never by any chance present to observe it. Everyone knows the story of that disastrous Paris production. The riotous hostility of Wagner's Parisian opponents, especially that of the aristocratic members of the Jockey Club ("whose right to consider themselves the rulers of the Grand Opera," wrote Wagner afterward, "I need not explain to you"), brought ruin to his hopes and plans. After those high-spirited connoisseurs had jeered and whistled through the second and third performances of *Tannhäuser,* Wagner withdrew his score. The offending opera vanished from the boards, and the corps de ballet was restored to its desired place and its rightful eminence.[2]

❦   ❦   ❦

[2] Wagner gives a detailed and trenchant account of the affair, written with quiet dignity and ironic humor, in his "Report on the Production of *Tannhäuser* in Paris," included in Vol. III of his collected Prose Works (translated by William Ashton Ellis: London, Kegan Paul, Trench, Trübner & Co., Ltd., 1907). See also the Memoirs of the Princess Metternich.

43

Those opera-goers who would test their realization of the effect of Wagner's return in later years to the work of his young manhood might try the experiment of listening with especial care, beginning at a particular point, the next time they hear a performance (in the opera house or by radio) of *Tannhäuser* as performed at the Metropolitan. The vigilant listener, following the performance with his score, will remember that for the Paris version of 1861 Wagner shortened the Overture of the Dresden version (that which is heard in full at concert performances when it is played alone, without the linked music of the Bacchanale). He omitted the last 154 measures, and ran the curtailed Overture directly into the revised and greatly extended [3] Bacchanale, without pause. Thus the listener to our supposititious opera performance will not hear the Overture's familiar "revivalistic close," as Tovey called it, with the return of the Pilgrims' chant accompanied by the persistent figure of the violins; nor will he hear it when the Overture and Bacchanale are played together.

He will find himself listening to music of

[3] In Peters's excellent uniform editions of the orchestral scores of the Dresden and Paris versions, the Bacchanale occupies 18 pages in the old version, 56 in the new; the scene between Venus and Tannhäuser fills 38 pages in the old version, 75 in the new. Together, the two scenes occupy 56 pages in the Dresden version, 131 in the Paris version.

44

the younger Wagner for almost three hundred
measures of the Overture. He should begin to
prick up his ears when the orchestra arrives at
the repetition of Tannhäuser's song in praise of
Venus, this time in E major (bar 243): for the
hearer is about to be precipitated from Wagner's
1840s into his far more adventurous 1860s. There
is an orchestral crash on the Sirens' motive, *molto
vivace;* and this is followed, fifteen measures
later, by a frenzied two-bar trill of the violins
on E.

From the next measure (bar 290) onward,
the hearer will notice that a marked change comes
over the music. It grows rapidly more intense,
more glowing and impassioned. The harmony is
richer, more complex, more chromatic; the melodies heard in the earlier part of the Overture are
more expressively treated. There are new themes.
One, a headlong and passionate figure for the first
violins in sixteenth-notes, may recall a passage
from the latter part of the Second Act of *Siegfried;* [4] another, heard soon after, seems to have
come, almost unmodified, out of *Tristan.* And the
instrumentation has suddenly caught fire, and is
burning and blazing like a cataract of flame.

At this point Wagner might have directed
that a sign be hung out, reading somewhat like
the notice in a playbill, "Fifteen years pass": we

[4] See note, page 101.

45

have left the relatively youthful and groping genius of 1845, and have come face to face with the adult and confident master of 1860, the resistless Wagner of *Tristan und Isolde:* the Wagner, in other words, who recomposed about one-third of *Tannhäuser*—for the eventual diversion of the Paris Jockey Club.

If one listens closely to this Paris version of the Bacchanale, one may hear Wagner grow suddenly in tonal stature and greatness before our ears. The Overture to *Tannhäuser* is a moving and beautiful work. But the Bacchanale is colossal and without a precedent. Nothing like this blazing torrent of orchestral tone had ever been released from a musician's imagination. Its overpowering intensity added a novel and perturbing page to the literature of music. Yet it would be a mistake to overlook the fact that Wagner in this music has, as usual, transfigured his subject-matter. The long decrescendo which ends the scene and introduces the dialogue of Venus and Tannhäuser contains some of the loveliest of Wagner's pages. A wise and discerning student of the work has reminded us that this Bacchanale is "no ordinary scene of sensual temptation, but Venus seems to have stepped from out the noble poem of Lucretius [5] in all her classic dignity. Conscious of her

[5] Lucretius in his poem, *De Rerum Natura,* begins with an apostrophe to Venus Genetrix, in which she is viewed as the creative force of Nature, the source of universal life and energy.

hidden power, she rests quietly and unconcerned, knowing that her supreme sovereignty can bridle the ungoverned tumult, until the handmaids of the goddess send forth her mandate and resolve the discord, turning the headlong passions to ordered love, and evolving from chaos a world of harmony. In the two cloud-pictures, we have not only a portrayal of the fabled love of gods for mortals, befitting the story of this union between man and a goddess; but also a far-reaching metaphor in which the story of the birth of order out of love is typified by Europa, and the story of the birth of beauty is symbolized by Leda, the mother of Helena."

So Wagner in this pagan Bacchanale, as always, leaves us thinking of everlasting things.

❧   ❧   ❧

The sensuous splendors of the Paris version of the Bacchanale may be heard not only in the opera house, but at many concert performances, for the work is in the repertoire of most American orchestras. It is not so easy to know the great scene between Venus and Tannhäuser that, in the opera, follows the Bacchanale. Yet it is here that the chief treasures of the revised score of *Tannhäuser* are to be found, in that impassioned dialogue wherein the Goddess of Love, with increasing seductiveness and urgency and despera-

tion, tries to detain at her side the minstrel who
has wearied of her charms, and who longs to return to that world which he once knew, with its
human creatures and its accustomed ways, its
sweet valleys blossoming with Spring, and the
music of its bells and birds and shepherds' pipes.
Portions of the old *Tannhäuser* survive in this
scene—as in the stanzas of the minstrel's song in
praise of Venus. But the larger part of the duet
gives us the mature and conquering Wagner of
the greater works.

Some of the most searching and exquisite
music that Wagner ever wrote—certainly the
most beautiful pages in *Tannhäuser*—are contained in this duet. There are, in particular, those
forty-seven measures in Venus's part, beginning
at "Wie hätt' ich das erworben," in which
Wagner wrote with a sorrowful intensity that
sends us, for comparison, to *Tristan* and *Parsifal*.
There is nothing to set beside this episode outside
Wagner's major works. It is not only beautiful
music, but it evokes for us, in two concentrated
bars—the sustained C-sharp for the voice on "O!
. . ." above the poignant interplay of the phrases
for violas and bassoon [6]—something of that
tragic Venus who is at the heart of Wagner's
conception, who is so strangely like his musically

[6] Beginning two bars before letter P in the Peters Edition
(1924) of the orchestral score.

unborn Kundry: this Venus, at once victorious and frustrate, who sees the death of love, "beautiful like the autumn evening, fading like the autumn evening," and knows the pain of an immedicable grief.

It was upon this scene, insipid, conventional, and trite in the earlier Dresden version, that Wagner lavished most prodigally the resources of his enriched and deepened art. "The only scene I mean to recast entirely," he wrote to Mathilde Wesendonck from Paris in 1860, "is that between Venus and Tannhäuser. I found Frau Venus stiff —a few good features, but no true life. I have added a fair number of verses . . . the Goddess of Delight herself has become affecting, and Tannhäuser's agony real, so that his invocation of the Virgin Mary bursts as a cry of anguish from his deepest soul. At that period [fifteen years before] I could never have made a thing like this. . . . It required a greater mastery, by far, which only now I have attained . . . At the time I wrote *Tannhäuser,* I was quite unable to portray the passionate inwardness, the full intensity, of woman . . . I've been compelled now to throw away almost everything in the [original] scene and build anew—in fact, I'm horrified at my former property-Venus! Well, it will be better this time . . . But the blithe and gay side of *Tannhäuser* is all good, and there I can alter

49

nothing: it has in it the distilled essence of everything that bears the flavor of the legend—although I have touched up features now and then . . ."

This scene between Venus and Tannhäuser, in the extended version, is still insufficiently valued by many lovers and students of Wagner. Those portions of the score of *Tannhäuser* which are not *Tannhäuser* at all, but repercussions of *Tristan* and anticipations of *Götterdämmerung* and *Parsifal,* are as yet relatively little known even to cultivated music lovers. One reason for this, perhaps, is that several of the most widely circulated editions of the vocal and orchestral scores of the opera contain only the early Dresden version. In none of these is there a word or a note to indicate to the innocent student the existence of any other version than the immature one that Wagner revised, transcended, and preferred. And in most of the standard analytical guides that are available in English, the *Tannhäuser* that is described is the old version, not the new. Furthermore, the principal part of the revised version, the duet between Venus and Tannhäuser, is seldom performed here in its entirety. What are perhaps the choicest of the pages that the post-*Tristan* Wagner added to the pre-*Tristan* version of *Tannhäuser* are habitually cut in many opera performances.

music underwent at the hands of the weariless Richard. In addition to those 131 pages in the revised score, he altered and compressed the scene of the Tournament of Song in the Second Act, omitting the song of Walther von der Vogelweide (for which he should receive a special blessing). He also rewrote the passage in the last scene of the First Act in which Tannhäuser, "deeply affected, throws himself into Wolfram's arms"— turning a feebly conventional violin figure into a fiery passage that vividly enforces the dramatic moment. He performed a similar operation upon the passage at the end of the Second Act (following the chorus of the Younger Pilgrims, heard offstage), where the passionately repentant Tannhäuser throws himself at Elisabeth's feet, kisses the hem of her garment, and then, "rising in the utmost agitation," exclaims "Nach Rom!" and rushes away. Those eight tumultuous measures for the violins and violas alone—an object-lesson in the art of treating intervals and rhythms—are a telling conversion of the "very tame violin passage" (as Wagner himself described it) which was all that the moment could press from his imagination and his technique in 1845. In the finale of the Third Act, he enriched the passage in which the Younger Pilgrims, bearing the miraculous green-leafed staff, enter the scene. And he made other changes of a minor character.

53

Altogether, the Appendix to the orchestral score in the Peters Edition which contains the altered passages of the Paris version comprises 155 pages, more than a third of the total number in the full score of the old version.

❦   ❦   ❦

Thus *Tannhäuser,* partly transformed, remains a thing unique among Wagner's works—unique, indeed, in opera. It is a hybrid, and in various ways it is a masterpiece. There is nothing to compare with the volcanic music of the Bacchanale, surely the most splendid and fearful eruption of sensual ecstasy and impassioned beauty in any art; and the duet that follows it is for the most part conceived and wrought in Wagner's greater manner.

Yet even without reference to the gorgeous addenda of the Paris version, even in those older portions of the score that represent the often-unregenerate Wagner of the Dresden days, there are many pages that satisfy and move us. It is easy to lose patience with the sentimentality, the baldness, the harrowing commonness of certain passages. We may not agree with the immortal Mr. Runciman that Tannhäuser's Hymn to Venus is "one of the world's greatest songs" (it is, I happen to believe, one of the world's worst); yet how fresh the bulk of the *Tannhäuser* music

54

is, how noble and dramatic in those passages wherein Wagner is not simply marking time while his inspiration lags; how deeply drenched with what he himself so aptly called "the legend's scent"! And, in the work's outstanding moments, we have at least two aspects of the greater Wagner: Wagner the enchanter, and Wagner the tragic poet.

Yes, it would be wise to think twice before classing among Wagner's lesser works this music-drama which is actually among his most elevated and most moving. *Tannhäuser* is a tragic parable of the endless conflict in the soul of man between those impulses which are earth-bound and sensual and those which are, as St. Paul described them, "the fruits of the spirit." The nobility of the music is irrepressible. Despite the occasional conventionality in the treatment, the suggestion of something that time has not left wholly unaffected, the music of Wolfram's monologue at the beginning of Act III persuades us, even in the light of Wagner's riper achievements, that we are listening to musical speech of genuine loftiness. And nowhere else in the whole course of his career as a musical dramatist did Wagner enforce a transition with such economy of means and certainty of effect as in that electrifying change, at Tannhäuser's invocation of the Virgin, from the sultry interior of the Venusberg, with its sensual fevers and its voluptuous mists, to the sweet clarity and sunlit peace of the Valley of the Wartburg, with the distant sound of sheep-bells and the Young Shepherd piping his bucolic lay.

❦   ❦   ❦

For many New Yorkers, the experience of a closer approach to the greatness of *Tannhäuser* will undoubtedly be associated for years with Lotte Lehmann's incarnation of the character of Elisabeth in recent performances at the Metropolitan Opera House. This Elisabeth is an embodiment of rare imaginative truth: the product, obviously, of a long and searching scrutiny of the character, and of a skillful synthesizing of its constituent factors, musical, dramatic, spiritual.

Mme. Lehmann's first entrance and her joyous greeting to the Hall of Song convey at once an impression of youthful charm and freshness and impulsiveness, a purity and an inner radiance of spirit, that are singularly affecting and singularly right.

When first I witnessed this performance, I found the word "virginal" in my mind and on my tongue; when I turned afterward to Wagner's own exposition of the character of his Elisabeth, I was not surprised to discover, though I had forgotten the fact, that he not only used that word, but that he described this noblest of the women

56

of his imaginative world in terms that might easily have been applied to Lotte Lehmann's re-creation—had Wagner been so fortunate as to witness it.

"The difficulty in the role of Elisabeth," he wrote, "is for an actress to give the impression of the most youthful and virginal unconstraint, without betraying how experienced, how delicate a womanly feeling it is that alone can fit her for the task." And elsewhere he says: "That actress alone can satisfy my aim, who is able to comprehend Elisabeth's piteous situation, from the first quick budding of her affection for Tannhäuser, through all the phases of its growth, to its final efflorescence as it unfolds itself in her Prayer—and to feel all this with a woman's finest sensibility."

No doubt Mme. Lehmann is familiar with Wagner's analysis of the character of Elisabeth; but it is one thing to know what an author wants you to do with his creation, and it is quite another thing to be able to fulfill his wishes. Mme. Lehmann accomplishes this unusual feat. She is, for a few enchanted hours, Wagner's Elisabeth: from the moment when she brings her before us as a tenderly affectionate and somewhat puzzled medieval princess, "whose sole reality had been her father and her chatelaine, and whose visions of the world were chiefly decorative: sentinels on the drawbridge, hunters assembling on the hillside—pictures hardly more real to her than those she weaves on her tapestry loom"—to that piteous culmination when she knows that happiness is forever closed to her, and she becomes the divine and humble penitent who, "having no sins of her own to do penance for, does penance for the sins of another."

Mme. Lehmann, by the truth and felicity of her histrionism, by the subtle dramatic expressiveness of her singing, makes actual for us this process of growth and evolution and denouement.

Thus she enhances the greatness of a work that remains, for all its inequalities and crudities and lapses, one of the landmarks in the progress of an inextinguishable genius toward his goal.

IV

From "Lohengrin" to "Das Rheingold"

WAGNER had scarcely completed the Dresden version of his *Tannhäuser* when he turned from that blemished and uneven work of genius and set to work upon another project, *Lohengrin,* the dramatic basis of which he outlined in the Summer of 1845, at Marienbad, where he had gone for a holiday and a cure. He tells us in *A Communication to My Friends* that in completing *Tannhäuser* he had been so "consumed with ardor" for his task that the nearer he approached its end, the more he was haunted by the fear that sudden death would stay his hand. (He was obsessed by the same fear, with better reason, while he was completing *Parsifal* many years later, burdened by the heart disease that killed him thirteen months after he had finished the scoring of the final scene). "When at last I wrote the closing chord of *Tannhäuser,*" he says, "I felt as joyful as though I had escaped some mortal danger."

So, on the forest-fringed slopes of Marienbad, with their healing, incomparable woods of pine, where even a Wagner might have been tempted to relax, the irrepressible Richard not only worked on his *Lohengrin* drama (which he had conceived in his wretched Paris days), but, as we shall note in a later chapter, dreamed of *Parsifal* and sketched a scenario for *Die Meistersinger*. Thus did Wagner take his ease.

It was only then, apparently, that the subject of *Lohengrin* took possession of him. He tells us that he "first learnt its story in connection with that of Tannhäuser." At that time, he says, "the tale indeed affected me, but did not prompt me to store the material for future use—not only because I was then completely saturated with [the character of] Tannhäuser, but also because the form in which Lohengrin first stepped before me made an almost disagreeable impression upon my feeling." He seems to have been disaffected by what he calls the "mystic twilight" that enwrapped the medieval poem. Later, at Marienbad, he saw it with unobscured simplicity and clarity, "as a noble expression of human longing . . . a genuine poem of the Folk." The impulse to deal with it became a dominating need, he says, despotic in its mastery over his imagination.

With the sketch for the *Lohengrin* drama in his portfolio, he returned from Marienbad to Dresden in August, 1845, in order to produce

Tannhäuser in the Autumn. During the following years he worked backward upon the music of *Lohengrin,* composing the Third Act first, the First Act next, the Second Act after that, and the Prelude last (in August, 1847). The orchestral score was finished in March, 1848.[1]

❦   ❦   ❦

A dozen years after he had completed *Lohengrin,* Wagner found it possible to say that the dramatic poem, as he restudied it, had touched him uniquely. In 1860 (the year in which the *Tristan* score was published) he wrote in a letter from Paris to Mathilde Wesendonck that he had been reading through a French prose translation of four of his opera texts, *The Flying Dutchman, Tannhäuser, Lohengrin,* and *Tristan.* He found that the poem of *Lohengrin* had especially affected him. "I cannot but hold it," he said, "to be the most tragic one of all"; and his "all," be it remarked, included *Tristan*—the poem, at least: he was not speaking of the music.

The tragic element of *Lohengrin* centres, obviously, in the character of Elsa. "The whole interest of *Lohengrin*," wrote Wagner in a famous essay,[2] "consists in an inner process within the mind of Elsa, involving every secret of the soul."

[1] *Lohengrin* was performed for the first time on August 28, 1850, at Weimar, under Liszt.

[2] *Zukunftsmusik.*

That process is unapparent in most embodiments of the part. Who of us has not suffered in the presence of the average Elsa of afflicting insipidity? Yet for Wagner himself, Elsa seems to have grown to extraordinary dimensions as he worked upon the evolution of the drama; and he wrote of her in later years as though he had almost come to regard her as its protagonist.

He has been speaking of the Lohengrin myth, and its symbolization of what he calls "the inmost essence of human nature, the necessity of love." He wonders what share in this longing the god and the mortal are to have, and he asks us to "marvel at the omnipotence of human minstrelsy, as it is unfolded in the simple mythos of the Folk, in which things that all our understanding cannot comprehend are laid bare." He describes, in mystical imagery, a vision that might be regarded as suggesting another aspect of the matchless Prelude to *Lohengrin,* minus the disclosure of the Holy Grail by the angelic host. "The ethereal sphere," he writes, "from which the god is yearning to descend to men, had stretched itself, through Christian longing, to inconceivable bounds of space. To the Hellenes, it was still the cloud-locked realm of thunder and the thunderbolt, from which the lusty Zeus moved down to mix with men in their own likeness. To the Christian, the blue firmament dissolved into an infinite sea of ecstasy, in which the forms of all the gods were melted, until at last it was the lonely image of his own person, longing Man, that alone was left to greet him from the ocean of his fantasy."

Then, later in the same essay, he turns his mind to Elsa: "This woman," he writes, with a kind of passionate intensity of worship, "this woman, who, with clear foreknowledge, rushes onward to her doom because of Love's imperative behest, who, amid the ecstasy of adoration, yet wills to lose her all: this woman, who, in her contact with Lohengrin, of all men, must founder, and, in doing so, must shipwreck her beloved too: this woman, who can love but thus and not otherwise, who, by the very outburst of her jealousy, wakes first from out the thrill of worship into the full reality of love, and by her act reveals its essence to him who had not fathomed it as yet: this glorious woman, before whom Lohengrin must vanish, because his own specific nature could not understand her—I had found her *now:* and the random shaft that I had shot towards the treasure, dreamt-of but hitherto unknown, was my own Lohengrin, whom now I must give up as lost; to track more certainly the footsteps of that true womanhood which should one day bring to me and all the world redemption, after manhood's egoism, even in its noblest form, had shivered into self-crushed dust before her."

The Elsa of Wagner is the rapt clairvoyant, the mystical dreamer, who, as she stands before her accuser and her judge, is a figure of spellbound and visionary absorption, for whom the world of her inward illumination is far more actual than the formidable reality of her situation. Her very first phrase, "Mein armer Bruder!" as she utters it abstractedly, speaking to herself, reveals her unmistakably. And later, as she stands on the balcony of the Kemenate in the coolness of the night and pours out her happiness upon the quiet air, we are made aware that this is part of that inner process which conditions the tragedy from its beginning to its end. Yet Elsa is likewise, as Wagner sees her, a figure of tragic grandeur and simplicity, ageless and universal—"the Spirit of the Folk," he calls her, "for whose redeeming hand I too, as artist and as man, was longing."

These complex yet universally symbolic figures are realized by Wagner with the loftiest poetic beauty in the drama of *Lohengrin*. I take leave to think that on the whole they are realized less completely in the music. Save for the lonely, unrivalled Prelude—in which the chief thematic material of the score is developed with a concentrated power and a splendor of genius that are

never equalled in the opera itself—*Lohengrin*
marks a decline in musical vitality from its immediate predecessor, the Dresden version of *Tannhäuser*. Granting its finer grain and more sensitive fabrication: granting its comparative absence
of those platitudes and banalities that afflict us in
many parts of *Tannhäuser:* granting the exceptional interest of certain pages in Ortrud's music
which betoken the greater Wagner who was to
come—granting all this, *Lohengrin* remains for
me a lesser work than *Tannhäuser*. I am aware
of its *longueurs,* which are not alleviated by the
metrical monotony of the writing, the sameness
of the rhythmic patterns throughout extensive
portions of the score, and that curious inflexi-
bility which qualifies at times the rapturous exaltation of the music.

❀ ❀ ❀

After the Spring of 1848, when Wagner finished the instrumentation of *Lohengrin,* he produced no music of consequence for more than five
years.[3] But he laid the foundations for the major
work of his life, the colossal *Ring des Nibel-
lungen,* the dramatic basis of which he planned
and worked out between 1848 and 1853 (the text
was privately printed early in the latter year);

[3] A few minor pieces written for the private edification of
the Wesendonck family belong to the year 1853.

and we know that the music which ultimately fulfilled that conception began to stir and germinate in him concurrently with the evolution of the drama.[4] Yet even so considerable a task as shaping the dramatic structure of the *Ring* did not exhaust his limitless energies, and Wagner was active with an appalling intensity during that musically uneventful period between March, 1848, when he finished the instrumentation of *Lohengrin,* and November 1, 1853, when he began the composition of *Das Rheingold.* In addition to evolving the four parts of the *Ring* drama, he occupied himself with various stage-works which were never completed; followed his profession as a musician; travelled; involved himself in a maladroit love affair; released a flood of writings on politics, sociology, ethics, aesthetics, together with explanatory programs, innumerable letters, and other by-products of his weariless brain. Forced into exile because of his part in the Dresden uprising of May, 1849, he settled in Zürich, met Mathilde Wesendonck (his Isolde of the coming years), and entered upon one of the most fruitful and momentous periods of creative activity in the history of any artist who has ever lived.

[4] In the Summer of 1850, Wagner went so far as to sketch the music for the Norn scene and for part of the following scene between Siegfried and Brünnhilde in *Siegfrieds Tod,* the drama which afterward became the *Götterdämmerung* of the *Ring.* Fortunately, he made no use of that premature attempt to speak the heroic language of the greater Wagner.

One morning in November, 1853, Wagner began to pace his study at Zürich, between the two writing-desks that he used—one high, at which he stood while drafting his preliminary sketches, and the other at which he sat during the phases of more leisurely development. The doorways were doorless, so that the restless music-maker could perambulate freely from room to room, in one of which stood a piano, for the trying over of effects. The overimaginative Praeger was mistaken, as we have long known, in asserting that Wagner "composed at the piano." He composed on his feet, or sitting at his desk, or lying on his divan; and he took no account of time, infuriating his wife Minna by keeping dinner waiting (the Wagners dined in the middle of the day). In the afternoon there were those "solitary walks in the mist" of which he speaks; and in the evening there were the young Isolde and her husband to call on at the Hôtel Baur au Lac. On that morning of November 1, 1853, he must have been especially engrossed in his workroom: for he had begun the music of *Das Rheingold*.[5]

The impulse to take up the actual composi-

[5] The music of *Das Rheingold* was composed between November 1, 1853, and January 14, 1854. The scoring was finished May 28th. The first performance, given against Wagner's wishes and in his absence, was at Munich, September 22, 1869—almost seven years before the work was heard in its proper place as the *Vorabend* of *Der Ring des Nibelungen*, at the first Bayreuth Festival, August 13, 1876.

tion of *Das Rheingold,* after what he described as "five years' arrest of my musical productiveness," had come to him shortly before in the course of a visit to Spezia, while he lay half-asleep and ill on a hotel bed. As Wagner afterward related the incident, he suddenly felt as though he were sinking in a flood of water: "The rush and roar took musical shape within my brain," he wrote, "in the form of the chord of E-flat major, surging incessantly in broken chords. These declared themselves as melodic figurations of increasing motion, yet the pure triad of E-flat major never changed. . . . I awoke from my half-sleep in terror, feeling as though the waves were now rushing high above my head. I at once recognized that the orchestral prelude to the *Rheingold,* which for a long time I must have carried about within me, yet had never been able definitely to fix, had at last come to being in me: and I quickly understood the very essence of my own nature—the stream of life was not to flow to me from without, but from within."

❀   ❀   ❀

Das Rheingold is ceaselessly fascinating to the student of Wagner because it marks the point at which the hampered genius who had written *Lohengrin* became the prodigal master who was to compose the *Ring.* We encounter here one of

68

the miracles in the history of the human brain. In 1848, in his thirty-fifth year, Wagner completed the scoring of *Lohengrin,* a nobly romantic work, streaked with genius, but incompletely realized. Somewhat more than five years later, this gifted music-maker had become, at forty, the most original musical mind in the art of his time, and was composing a score without precedent or model. The Wagner of *Lohengrin* had become the Wagner of *Das Rheingold.* A chasm between two different worlds had been bridged, and a new master had been born.

The Wagner of *Lohengrin* could not have conceived this music, would not have ventured it. And we are in a new world of the imagination, as well as a new world of inspiration and of craftsmanship. Wagner had attempted no such range of evocation in his earlier works; nor had the art of music before his time dared to conceive so vast a canvas. With *Das Rheingold* had been born not only a new master and a new imaginative world, but a new art of tones, mage-like, Promethean, sustained by a divine effrontery.

This is not to say that in *Das Rheingold* we find the completely matured Wagner, full-fledged and unqualified. *Das Rheingold* is transitional. In the same year that Wagner finished it, he began the music of *Die Walküre;* and we have only to set that score beside the score of *Rheingold* to

69

realize the unbelievable speed with which Wagner's style developed and ripened after his fortieth year. In the music of *Rheingold* the touch is still at times a bit uncertain, the handling of those wonderful themes that had come to him—who knows just when?—is still occasionally tentative and a little timid. Consider, for instance, the difference between his treatment of the Flight and Freia motives in *Rheingold* and the superb assurance and resourcefulness with which he uses them in *Die Walküre*. Nor has the music of *Rheingold* the harmonic pregnance, the breadth of melodic span, the grasp of structure, the freedom of stride and sweep of gesture that we find in *Die Walküre*—the Wagner of *Rheingold* was still not quite the Olympian figure who was striding toward him through the mountain mists.

Yet this is only to note degrees of imaginative splendor and beauty. Wagner, as Romain Rolland said, carried all Nature in his imagination; and in the music of *Rheingold* we get for the first time the Wagner who released without stint his delight and exhilaration in the fascination of the natural world. The music of *Das Rheingold,* Prologue to the titanic *Ring,* begins in the abyss, in the twilight depths of the timeless river. It ends with lightning and a rainbow and a stormy, tragical, deceptive sunset brightening the faces of the doomed gods; and between, there is music of fire and clouds and mountain heights and subterranean gloom, and the roar of wind among primeval hills, and the gathering tempests and the never-absent sense of the wonder and strangeness of the created earth.

Scattered up and down the pages of the score are innumerable strokes of genius: music full of dramatic power and tonal loveliness and heroic beauty; and at times we hear the voice and feel the earth shake under the tread of the gigantic Wagner of the later works—Wagner almost at his mightiest.

"Wagner called himself the 'twilight man' [*Dämmermann*]," wrote Frau Wesendonck, years after, concerning the *Rheingold* days at Zürich. "In the hour between five and six he used to call and try over on my grand piano what he had composed in the morning. It was delightful to see his features light up as he sat down to the instrument, though when he entered the room he was visibly tired and exhausted. At times it would happen that something did not satisfy him. Such was the case with the construction of the Valhalla motive in *Rheingold*. 'That is good, Master!' I exclaimed as he played it for me. 'No, no!' he replied, 'it must become still better.' For a while he strode impatiently up and down the room, then left hurriedly. The following day he did not appear, nor the second day, nor the third. Then, on

71

the fourth day, he came in quietly, sat down to the piano and played the glorious theme precisely as it was before. 'You were right,' he remarked; 'I can't improve it.' "

No one could have improved it. No one could have improved the really great things in *Rheingold*. It is not possible to think of an enhanced expression of the imaginative conception that underlies, for example, the Valhalla theme. It has been said there once for all, finally, exhaustively. The idea and the music are inseparable. The stronghold of the gods, the majestic castle gleaming in the dawn upon the height across the valley, is what Wagner's imagination saw; it is what the music pictures.

But the music does more than that. It turns the specific and the temporal into the universal and the never-ending. Those great triads in D-flat, with their foundational simplicity and their elemental grandeur, their nobility of pace and contour, embody, through some mystery of the creative will, "the Thing behind the Thing"—the essence of serenely epic beauty, of godly serenity and dignity and strength; and we who listen are, for a fortunate brief instant, touched, like the music, with the divine illusion of immortality.

This theme, and others in the *Ring,* have almost the character of everlasting things: one

72

fancies that they must always have been—that
Wagner simply came upon them, ageless, completely shaped, unchangeable in power and expressiveness, at some turning in his creative path.
They seem almost to have been coexistent with
the elemental or imponderable realities that they
symbolize and evoke: water, fire, wind, light; wisdom and destiny; majesty and youth; hatred,
ecstasy, loveliness; a gnome's malice or a god's
despair.

We feel this often in listening to *Rheingold*.
Its motives that capture the essence of youth and
all delight, the renewal of strength and beauty—
Freia's theme; the theme of the Golden Apples;
and, for contrast, the dark music of Alberich and
the Nibelungs; and, yet again, those other themes
of portent and of destiny, those that are associated with the rape of the Ring, with Erda, her
warnings and her prophecies; and, finally, that
music in which Wagner compasses the sublime:
the music of Valhalla at the opera's end, glorious
in the evening light: these things are marvels of
the projective imagination. They have a fullness
of statement, an inevitability, that nothing in the
earlier Wagner had suggested—save only in two
instances: in those musical anomalies, the Overture to *The Flying Dutchman* and the Prelude
to *Lohengrin*.

What all this means is that, during the years in which Wagner's musical activities were virtually suspended, his imagination and his technique underwent an almost unbelievable enhancement. Wagner in 1853 had ceased to be merely a composer of enormous potentialities, and had become one of the two or three excelling geniuses of music.

Prior to 1853 he could never have conceived or accomplished such a piece of imaginative and technical audacity as that which he coolly pulls off at the very outset of *Rheingold*. Hearing that amazing Prelude, in which Wagner dared to build a symphonic movement of 136 measures upon the chord of E-flat major, we realize that the Wagner of *Tannhäuser,* of *Lohengrin,* could not possibly have done this, would not have attempted it. Neither Bach nor Beethoven ever did anything quite so daring as to construct an entire movement in slow tempo on a single chord. Monteverde's little experiment in *Orfeo* two and a half centuries before was merely a hint to the infinitely greater musician.

It is in the music of *Das Rheingold* that the essential Wagner—the Wagner who most profoundly stirs us—first reveals himself. He himself has told us that with *Das Rheingold* he was venturing his foot on a new path. One may doubt whether he himself realized how new it was. The

Wagner who set himself to the composition of this score had left behind him forever the formulas of *Tannhäuser* (in its older version) and of *Lohengrin*—their often thick-fingered style, their frequent heavy-footedness, their monotony of rhythm and of metre, their harmonic and melodic conventionalities. In *Rheingold* he discloses a new heaven and a new earth, breathes a new air; and we, who are privileged to accompany him, share his exhilaration.

The Wagner of *Rheingold* is an artist and an enchanter such as music had not known. Nothing in the least like this score had ever come from the hand of a musician. Its Spring-like quality, its fresh and limpid beauty, its magnificent spaciousness and power, its simplicity touched with magic, its splendor of imagery and distinction of style, are fused into a novel and surprising unity.

In *Rheingold,* as in all his later scores, he sets music to its essential task: its work of completion and fulfillment. Here, time after time, we encounter music that exhausts an imaginative concept, says the ultimate thing of it, distills its essence. The idea and its embodiment coalesce. *Das Rheingold* is full of such things. It is the first of Wagner's scores in which the tone-poet and the craftsman are fused and coöperative. We are not yet face to face with Wagner the consum-

mate master. *That* Wagner is still to be revealed.
We shall hear him in *Die Walküre*. But *Das
Rheingold* remains a thing apart, a thing of unfailing loveliness and refreshment, with its visions
of earth and sky, its gods and earth-men ascending and descending through its tonal cosmos, and
its river-maidens lamenting at the close their rav-
ished Gold. ❦ ❦ ❦

It is always a curiously moving experience
to hear *Das Rheingold* again after a lapse of time
—especially at the beginning of a complete performance of the *Ring*. One listens to its unfading
themes as they appear in their pristine form; and
one thinks ahead to the manifold processes of
transmutation that they are to undergo in the
course of the Tetralogy, as Wagner's genius,
maturing as the work itself matures, weaves them
into the constantly enriched and expanding fabric
of his vast design. One sees in the distant *Götterdämmerung,* which Wagner was not to complete
for twenty years, the crown and consummation
of the all-embracing tragedy: its wrongs atoned
for, its gods and heroes dead, Valhalla in flames,
Brünnhilde an imperishable memory in the falling
dusk, and the Ring returned to those violated
depths from which its Gold so long before was
stolen.

In *Rheingold* all this is yet to come. One

listens as the themes emerge, reflections of enduring things; and one seems to be attending at the
birth of some universe of the inner mind. One
does not think of these themes as invented by
Wagner, as deliberately composed: they seem like
other aspects of the things they signify: as their
equivalents in that fourth dimension of reality
which is the world of the creative will.

In the music of *Rheingold* these manifesta-
tions have a quality and a character that are their
own. For it is one of the signals of Wagner's
genius that each of his works is steeped in its
own peculiar essence, lives in a world that is its
own, conditioned by its events, colored by the
moods that shaped its spirit. In *Rheingold,* one
of these traits is an enchanting clarity of musical
conception. A pure and delicious air blows out of
the dawn behind Valhalla. The beauty of the
music has often a captivating lucidity, simplicity,
directness. It has also an unclouded serenity and
sweetness. In none of Wagner's subsequent works
has he given us such music as that tranquil C
major passage for the violins above the quiet
ostinato of the timpani that accompanies the
gradual clearing of the air after the departure
of the vanquished and raging Alberich, as Wotan
stands absorbed in contemplation of the Ring that
has already doomed him. Yet there is room in

Das Rheingold for music of another sort: for the
dark mysteriousness that shrouds the motive of
the Norns as it ascends in the muted horns and
violas, accompanying the warning words of Erda
the seeress, "Wie alles war, weiss ich." . . .

❦   ❦   ❦

With *Rheingold* we begin the cycle of that
quadruple work which is far and away the most
tremendous product of the creative imagination
and the organizing will ever achieved by any artist. Admittedly, the hand of its creator has fal-
tered, for a moment, here and there; but so, it
will probably be conceded, has the mightier hand
that shaped humanity and the flawed and treacherous earth.

This cosmic drama of the musical mind, this
Ring of Wagner's, is not only the hugest thing
that was ever attempted by the creative will: it is
also, in the ultimate sense of the word, the greatest. Only the *Divina Commedia* and Goethe's
Faust and some of the Greek plays can be compared with it. And for range and power of expression, Wagner's Tetralogy stands alone.

No wonder the sense of this transcendent
greatness overwhelms us as we sit in the presence
of *Das Rheingold,* and hear the stirring of the
depths, and know that at the close of *Götterdäm-*

merung, with the vast tragedy played to its predestined end, the immemorial river will be flowing quietly beneath the distant, ruined stronghold
of the gods—a symbol of man's supremacy over
destiny and time.

V

"Die Walküre"

BRÜNNHILDE sleeps!—I, alas, still wake!"
wrote Wagner to Liszt on New Year's
Day, 1855, announcing the completion of the
composition-drafts of *Die Walküre,* which he
had finished December 27th.[1] That blend of
exultation and despondency was characteristic of
the harassed musician in those difficult Zürich
days. Tormented by ill-health (his old enemy,
erysipelas), and by his inexorable creditors, he
meditated darkly, like his own Wotan, upon *das
Ende.* Hans von Bülow wrote to Alexander Ritter in August, 1854,—while Wagner was in the
midst of the First Act of *Die Walküre,*—that he
had received bad news from Zürich. "He is much
worried, and gloomy enough to shoot himself."
Wagner himself flirted with the idea of death as
he gave life to immortal music. "How often I'm
heartily sick of living!" we find him writing to
Praeger after his futile London expedition in the

[1] He did not complete the instrumentation until the Spring
of 1856. *Die Walküre* was first performed, without Wagner's
consent, at Munich, on June 26, 1870. It was given as Part II of
Der Ring des Nibelungen on August 14, 1876, at the first Bayreuth
Festival.

80

Spring of 1855—though perhaps he would not have embraced the Gray Henchman as warmly as he thought if the opportunity had come. His wretchedness was genuine enough, in all conscience; but the creative impulse blazed or smouldered so unquenchably in the man's spirit that his despairs often became unreal even to himself. In the very next sentence of his letter to Praeger we find him exclaiming: "This splendid Nature —this glorious Alpine world—is attuning me to life once more; so I've taken up my work again."

That "work," so casually alluded to, was the instrumentation of *Die Walküre,* which he had composed the year before within a period of six months—between June 28 and December 27, 1854.

"You are to have the *Rheingold,*" he wrote to Liszt from Zürich on June 14, 1854, "but you shall not set eyes on it till it is in the worthy form I contemplate; and I shall make no progress with it [on the "fair copy" of the orchestral score] till after many leisure hours in the long Winter evenings; for I cannot delay over it now—I must set to work on *Die Walküre,* which I am gloriously full of . . ." He was indeed "gloriously full" of it—consumed by a fury of creative passion. He set down the music of the enormous work in his composition-sketch at a staggering rate of speed: the First Act in a little over nine weeks, the Second Act in less than eleven weeks, the Third Act in thirty-eight days. No wonder its completion had "terribly exhausted" him, as he wrote to Dr. Pusinelli.

❧ ❧ ❧

What strikes us first as we come upon *Die Walküre* in our advance through Wagner's works is the superhuman power and stride and stature of the tone-poet whom this score reveals. The Wagner who speaks from this music has become a Titan of art, riding the storms like his own cloud-sweeping Donner, a brother of wind and flame, with all the Spring in his voice and the ancient mysteries of destiny and death shadowing his eyes.

The history of Wagner's creative activity presents us with three striking instances of abrupt and inexplicable transition. Wagner, as we have seen, expressed his own astonishment at the transformation wrought in his creative processes between the composition of *Rienzi* and that of *The Flying Dutchman*. But even more remarkable, as we see it from this distance, was the transformation of the romantic Wagner of *Lohengrin* into the epic wonder-worker of *Das Rheingold*. What happened to that astonishing brain between 1848 and 1853? And what was it that turned the composer of *Das Rheingold* into the composer of *Die Walküre?* The two works were separated by only a month's interval: Wagner finished the scoring of *Rheingold* on May 28, 1854; on June 28th he began the composition of *Die Walküre.*[2] He rose from the completion of *Das Rheingold* with a whole new world of the imagination spread about him, but with his powers still incompletely developed and applied. Thirty-one days later he sat down to compose *Die Walküre,* and the first measures that he wrote disclosed a consummate master, writing with absolute certainty of style and fullness of power. Here, for the first time in Wagner's evolution, is a demonstration of the great creative and organizing genius of the later works, the first sweep of the mighty arm over an immeasurable canvas.

"The *Walküre* music is started," he wrote to Liszt in July. "My! how the thing begins to hum!" William Ashton Ellis, Wagner's English biographer, interprets this remark as meaning that "the *Rheingold* music was a mere preliminary when compared with the *Walküre* music that he had just commenced." Whether Wagner meant quite that or not, Mr. Ellis's statement of the case is not essentially unjust. *Das Rheingold* is a wonderful work, a work of enchanting beauty and

[2] According to Dr. Otto Strobel's authoritative article, *Die Kompositionskizzen zum "Ring des Nibelungen,"* in the *Bayreuther Festspielführer* for 1930 (pp. 114-122).

originality and enduring fascination—a truth to
which I have tried to bear witness in the preceding chapter of this book. But it would be idle to
deny that it lacks the supreme felicity of style and
the mastery of tonal speech and tonal structure
which in this instance seem to have entered almost overnight into Wagner's equipment as an
artist.[3]

We need not search long in order to be convinced that in *Die Walküre* the tremendous Wagner has at last arrived—and with startling sud-
denness. Think back to *Rheingold,* to the passage
shortly before the end, in which Donner the
Thunder God draws the storms to a head. The
Donner theme, as the god sings to it his summoning cry in B-flat, with the instruments of the
brass choir taking it up in turn, under swirling
clouds of the divided strings, gives Wagner, as
John Runciman observes, "his great chance"; and
Wagner makes much of it. But it is not easy to
agree with Runciman that this *Rheingold* storm
shows us "Wagner in the plenitude of his power."
For that exhibition we must look to *Die Walküre.*

Turn to the opening pages of *Die Walküre,*

[3] Certain familiar motives in the *Ring* were conceived years
before the composition of the scores as we know them. But
Wagner, guided by a generally infallible artistic instinct, did not
undertake the organization of his greater scores until Nature had
seen that he was ready for the task. He seems to have been ripe
for the creation of the *Walküre* score precisely when he began it.

to the brief prelude in which the orchestra depicts the storm of rain and hail that beats upon the roof of Hunding's forest dwelling. Again we hear the Donner theme—as before, merely a bugle call surprisingly transformed. We hear it first on the tubas, after the rain and wind of the long string tremolo on D have risen to a turbulent fortissimo. But only the theme remains the same. What Wagner does with it is the thing to note. We are aware at once of a power and sweep of gesture, a freedom of movement, a significance and weight of utterance, that were not apparent in the earlier work. Here, for the first time, there is complete assurance, resourcefulness, superb dominion over the material in hand.

Note what the magician can do now with his harmonies, his rhythms, his instruments; with the old devices of pedal-point and canon. Hear him take that fragment of the D minor scale with which he started off under the persistent, rain-soaked, wind-beaten tremolo of the violins and violas, and make titanic music by setting it in canonic imitation for the strings and wind, with the Donner theme in the brass asserting itself more and more mightily through the fury of the orchestral storm. Notice how, by the use of the dissonance of the minor-second, he gains a new intensity and drive. Mark how swiftly he works up the movement to its climax, and how soon and craftily he is done with it, and is passing on to the succeeding mood. It is all over in one hundred and ten measures, and in less than two minutes' time; but in that brief interval the gigantic strength and surety of the thing have made us feel the might that can be exerted by a musical imagination of the first order, working at white heat. And let it be observed that Wagner has given us here something more than mere musical tone-pointing. This Prelude has an independent and self-contained life. It is not only a magnificent tone-picture, but a mountainous piece of music.

❧ ❧ ❧

It is in *Die Walküre* that Wagner, for the first time in the *Ring,* makes us aware of the vastness of the issues with which he is concerned. The work embodies two concurrent actions. The major one is the overarching and superhuman drama involving the consequences of Wotan's sin, stretching backward to *Das Rheingold* and to the theft of the Ring, and forward to the cosmic tragedy of doom and expiation that will be consummated in *Götterdämmerung*. The other drama is the human and subsidiary one of Siegmund and Sieglinde.

Coming to *Die Walküre* after *Das Rheingold,* the hugeness and daring of its scope are bound to be overpowering. Yet when we see the

86

work steadily and see it whole, we realize that there is not a measure or a word too much. From the breaking of the storm that drives the hunted Siegmund to seek shelter beneath his foeman's roof, to that last incomparable tableau of the sleeping Valkyr behind her towering wall of flame, there is no step in the progress of the drama that is not vitally relevant to what has gone before and what is still to come.

Anton Seidl, Wagner's assistant at Bayreuth and one of his earlier and major interpreters in America, estimated that there are a million notes in the score of *Die Walküre;* and throughout that densely woven tissue of vocal and instrumental speech there is not a phrase that does not spring from the central conception of the tonal dramatist. There is not a moment's swerving from the lofty and impassioned tragedy of the poet's scheme, nor a break in the fabric of the musician's intricate design. That is why such unabridged perform-ances as the Metropolitan vouchsafes us on the special and quasi-festival occasions of its Wagner Cycles are so richly contributive to our under-standing and appreciation of Wagner's work.

In *Die Walküre* there is no demand upon Wagner's expressional capacity to which it is un-equal. He can "spring imagination with a phrase." His insight and his powers can now unlock for his imagination every secret of the inner and the outer world save those profoundest ones of all which were reserved for the composer of *Tristan* and of *Parsifal*. Nowhere does this music falter or weaken in its obedience to the tone-poet's will. It can voice the deep simplicities of feeling as well as those mysteries of which we cannot speak in words. Yet everywhere within that horizon-leaping range the music speaks the mind and purpose of its begetter with uncanny fullness and precision and subduing eloquence. Wagner would show you Brünnhilde wrapping her tenderness as a garment about the anguished and defeated god who is her father; and in the phrase of ineffable beauty that she sings to him —so simple, so unsought—"What were I, should I cease to be thy will?" there is epitomized the whole of selfless love. And later, when the musician would evoke the image of Brünnhilde the Valkyr, the Messenger of Fate, unearthly bright, appearing before the doomed Siegmund in the mountain dusk, the solemn chanting of the brass is freighted with the mysterious majesty of death.

It is this that makes *Die Walküre* so peculiarly significant in Wagner's career as an artist: it was the first of his scores in which his powers as a musician were completely adequate to the task that his imagination as dramatist and poet had set for them. It is easy to imagine him returning in afteryears to the subject of one of his ear-

lier operas and making a new, unrecognizable
thing of it. Indeed, he gave us a sample of what
might have been when, as the matured composer
of *Tristan und Isolde,* he returned to the *Tannhäuser* that he had completed fifteen years before,
and lavished on its first two scenes the subtlety
and power of his ripened art. Imagine the drama
of *Tannhäuser* recomposed throughout by the
author of *Tristan!* Imagine, too, a *Lohengrin* rewritten in the sixties! But a recomposed *Walküre*
is unthinkable. And this is the first of Wagner's
scores of which that could be said. It marked the
beginning of his period of full command over the
stuff of his imagination and the materials of his
art. Thenceforward his speech was commensurate
with his purpose, his vision, and his will.

※   ※   ※

We come from a performance of *Die Walküre,* as of any other among Wagner's greater
works, with a sense of dazed and shaken incredu-
lity, the conviction that we have experienced some
capturing of essences, some projection of reality
that transcends art: for we are in the presence
of one among those few supreme artists who have
seized "an eternal moment in which they have
rested—who have stood still with time, halted
upon the threshold of night and day."

Wagner seems to have felt something of this

while he was at work upon certain pages in his scores. Writing to the Princess Caroline Sayn-Wittgenstein in November, 1854, during his pre-occupation with the music of *Die Walküre,* he told her how the thing had racked him. "It affects me far too painfully," he said. "Truly, there is not a sorrow in the world that does not find here its most agonizing expression. . . . I became quite ill over it several times, and had to give it up." And then he added: "I am now in Act II, at the scene where Brünnhilde appears to Siegmund to tell him he must die—one scarcely can call this kind of thing 'composition'!"

One scarcely can. Wagner might justifiably have said of such unexplained achievements of the creative will as the scene he mentions, and of many others that he might have mentioned, what Dante says in the *Purgatorio:* "Think, Reader, if within myself I marvelled, when I beheld the thing itself stand still, and in its image it transformed itself." For we are here in a region of the imagination where our instruments of registration and assessment are too blunt to serve. Like Dante, we can only marvel, as Wagner marvelled (so he tells us), again and again at the things that he found himself recording. It is the recognition that we are in the presence of some such demonstration as this that makes our experience of Wagner so different from any other that music can give us.

The scene of which Wagner spoke—that scene of exalted pathos in which Brünnhilde, the deputy of Wotan and of death, comes to Siegmund in the darkening pass to tell the chosen hero of his summons to Valhalla and the high company of the gods: how often we have sat before it, in dozens of performances of *Die Walküre,* good, bad, and terrible, yet how unfailingly it overwhelms us!

It is not difficult to understand how this aspect of *Die Walküre,* in particular, must have affected Wagner. As a man, Wagner was sometimes deficient in sensitivity; yet in all music there is no tenderness like his. As a music-maker, he can be tender without excess or falsity. Throughout the reaches of his later works there is never a sentimental lapse. He is tender as are the wise and piteous and contained.

The tenderness that speaks from the music of *Die Walküre* is a thing peculiar to that work. There is deep and impassioned tenderness in the passages between Siegmund and Sieglinde; but I am thinking rather of the music that Wagner has written for Brünnhilde and for Wotan, with its accent that belongs to otherworldly beings, its moods that are an elevation and enlargement of our own.

Repeatedly in *Die Walküre* this peculiar quality comes over the music and gives it an in-

estimable beauty and nobility. Turn to the opening
of the scene between Brünnhilde and the defeated
Wotan in the Second Act, and refresh your memory of the A major passage beginning at Brünnhilde's words, "Zu Wotan's Willen sprichst du,"
accompanied pianissimo by the horns over a pedal
E of the basses—that passage to which I have
referred before. After a hundred hearings, some
of us cannot listen with composure to the wonderful phrase, "Wer bin ich, wär' ich dein Wille
nicht?" sung over the quietly dropping sixths of
the horns, with the indescribable rise of the voice
to C-sharp at "dein Wille." A child could read
the passage; but only Wagner could have written it.

Above all, this superearthly tenderness trans-
figures with sublimity the great Farewell and its
orchestral epilogue—that music, so mercilessly
hackneyed, which still turns the heart to water
by its imaginative truth and its insupportable
beauty. We may search through Wagner's other
scores and we shall find no music that moves us
quite as this does.

There is a subtle and searching comment implicit in that well-nigh forgotten novel, *Evelyn
Innes,* at the point where Evelyn, the famous
Wagnerian prima donna, pleading on her knees
before her father for forgiveness of her sin, finds
herself singing the very phrases of Brünnhilde's

supplication in her final scene with Wotan: "the celebrated phrase, so plaintive, so full of intercession, broke from her lips, 'Was my offence so deep in disgrace that thou dost plan so deep a disgrace for me?' . . . She knelt at her father's or at Wotan's feet—she could not distinguish; all limitations had been razed. She was *the* daughter at *the* father's feet."

Here, in the scene of Wotan's Farewell, as in all of Wagner's later writing, is music that meets the ultimate test; for it selects a universal theme, the immemorial sorrow of farewell and loss, and treats it with exalting greatness and consummate truth. Wagner had already given us "the daughter at the father's feet." Now he gives us, in essence, the most ancient and common of human griefs: the grief of parting and separation —the separation that is terrible in its finality, in the desolation that it foresees.

Yet observe that this so-human music is of superhuman loftiness and grandeur. We are in a world where sorrow has become majestic, equable, and strong, "commending grave thoughts, thoughts lasting to the end." We know that if we could witness the anguish of a god, we should find that this music of Wagner's would seem the fitting, inevitable expression of our mood.

❋   ❋   ❋

A performance of *Die Walküre* is always an event, no matter how routine the playing. Before that concisely magnificent piece of storm music which begins the score has reached its climax, we know that great matters are under way; and this conviction of momentousness never leaves us until the close, and we are released from Wagner's thronging and cumulative marvels. Yet the work rewards unstintedly a major performance of any one among its leading roles. The Wotan of the Metropolitan's Friedrich Schorr, for example, has an integrity of purpose and effect that ranks it among the noblest Wotans within the memory of most New Yorkers of today—with Fischer's, with van Rooy's. Mr. Schorr outdoes himself especially in his comprehension and delivery of that narration of Wotan's to Brünnhilde in the Second Act which Wagner regarded as indispensable to the unfolding of the *Ring*. He told Liszt that at one time he came almost to the point of wanting to discard this scene entirely. He was, he said, afraid of it: "a thing like this," he remarked with a bitterness not wholly unforgivable, "is written only for such as have some staying power—that is, for no one!" Happily, he changed his mind about discarding the scene. He took up the draft again and went through it, he says, "with all the necessary expression." He found by this means that his misgivings were unjustified, and that, on the contrary, "the appropriate rendering produced a truly musical and enthralling effect."

One can scarcely be too grateful to him. The scene is monumental as a tour de force of musico-dramatic psychology, in which the mind and motivation of Wotan are laid bare. It is not only essential to a comprehension of *Die Walküre,* but it makes clear the inner structure of the *Ring.*

We cannot know the full extent of Wotan's tragedy unless we hear in its entirety this crucial narrative in the Second Act, which is far more than a mere recital of the events of *Rheingold,* as some have thoughtlessly asserted. For this narrative—"the most important scene in the entire *Ring*," as Wagner called it—is actually Wotan's revelation to Brünnhilde of his tragic destiny, looking not only backward, but far into the future: discerning, in the seeds that have been sown, the inescapable end. It is a baring of his mind and will and soul, a disclosure of an essential part of that interior dramatic action which is Wagner's true concern. We have not reached the core of *Die Walküre* unless we have heard that agonized cry of Wotan's, "Was ich liebe, muss ich verlassen!"

This scene has acquired a new vitality at the Metropolitan in recent years through Mr. Schorr's significant treatment of its dramatic and musical elements in the uncut performances

95

of *Die Walküre* that are part of the yearly cycle. From the intimacy and tragic quietness of the opening phrases of the narrative, which Mr. Schorr so skillfully achieves, to the terrific climax in which the fragments of Wotan's ruined cosmos shatter the god's despairing dream, he makes us realize what Wagner meant by saying that this was the most significant passage in the *Ring*. And, in the culminating Farewell, I have heard no other Wotan who gave to "freier als ich, der Gott!" the deeply tragic significance with which Mr. Schorr endues the phrase.

Wotan, beyond question, is the cardinal figure of the *Ring*—even though he does not appear at all in its concluding drama, and only under an alias in *Siegfried*. Yet it is not Wotan, nor any other male character, in the *Ring* or elsewhere, who is Wagner's chief creation. Wagner as an artist was a feminist all his life; and when the time arrives for a final assessment of his genius, it will be recognized, I think, that his most triumphant achievement was his creation of the great women who inhabit his imaginative world. They are all great in their respective ways, and there is none to match them in the other arts save in Euripides, in Shakespeare, in Meredith.

Brünnhilde, Isolde, Senta, Elisabeth, Sieglinde—they walk in light and loveliness and wisdom and exaltation and heroic beauty. Like

Diana, they make that which is about them seem like the dust around the blaze of jewels. Wonder lives in them. They move like dawn or mountain winds across "the largeness of the evening earth"; and not time, but eternity, has whispered in their ears.

Perhaps the most magical of Wagner's women is Sieglinde. She is not the greatest, but she haunts us longest. Like the Iphigenia of Euripides, she is passionate and tender, simple and complex, reckless and wise, strong and weak, heroic and shrinking; and her purity is as elemental as her passion. She is difficult to re-create upon the stage, probably for the reason that no other one of Wagner's women is so bafflingly simple, at once so complex and direct.

No singing-actress of our time has achieved a more telling and veracious Sieglinde than Lotte Lehmann's. It gives us the essentials of the character, this remarkable and deeply touching embodiment of Mme. Lehmann's. It gives us Sieglinde's tenderness, her passion and her essential purity, her resolution, her impulsiveness, her shrinking pathos and her steel-like strength. She is warm and pitiful, enraptured and faltering. She stands before us touched with the mystery and the remoteness and the heroic simplicity of the Sagas. In certain moments of salient exactness and felicity of suggestion, she colors her voice and shapes her gestures with something of the strangeness and wonder of those who were daughters of earth in old, forgotten, far-off times, and heard Spring waters running through primeval woods, and drove wild flocks across the twilit hills.

It is one of the marks of Mme. Lehmann's Sieglinde that she is most piercing when the music is. I have quoted in this chapter the passage from one of Wagner's letters, written while he was composing *Die Walküre,* in which he speaks of the agonizing utterances of sorrow that this score contains—"I have had to pay for the expression of these sorrows," he remarks parenthetically. Mme. Lehmann's delivery of Sieglinde's music in her frenzied scene with Siegmund in the Second Act makes us realize with peculiar vividness what Wagner must have meant. In such measures as those that echo the baying of Hunding's pursuing hounds in the eight terrible chords of the horns and trumpets, and Sieglinde's "Wo bist du, Siegmund?" she charges the music with an almost insupportable intensity of tragic woe.

But if Sieglinde is the most magical of Wagner's women, Brünnhilde is beyond comparison the greatest. It is in *Götterdämmerung* that she towers most overwhelmingly; but it is in *Die Walküre*—especially in the unabbreviated form of the work that the Metropolitan gives us in its cyclic performances—that she comes closest to us. We cannot know all that Brünnhilde's supplication is unless we have heard, and have remembered, certain passages in it that the shortened version of the opera customarily elides—especially those measures, sung above persistent sixteenth-note figures in the strings, wherein Brünnhilde reveals to Wotan the secret springs of her pity and her guilt. "Mein Aug' erschaute, was tief im Busen das Herz zu heil'gem Beben mir traf," sings Kirsten Flagstad: and when the extraordinary voice moves through those descending intervals above the poignant phrases of the violins and 'celli and violas, we know that we have looked within the open heart and heard the veritable pleading of Brünnhilde.

For Mme. Flagstad, when she sings Brünnhilde in *Die Walküre,* stands at the re-creative center of its performance, and makes it what Wagner evidently wished it to be. The utter humility of her voice as she submits herself to Wotan's wrath; the purity and exaltation of the rising phrase to the long-held E that is the climax of her revelation of Wotan to himself—such things as these become for us, as we listen, inseparable from the work of art itself. "Der diese Liebe . . ." she sings, and the music becomes articulate with everything that selfless love can

99

mean, and all that a great creative genius could say of it in a special moment of inspiration.

Such things prepare us fittingly for the Finale, which is like no other in all music, with its unforgettable picture of Loge's crimson fires leaping against the blue-black sky and brightening the armor of the quiet figure underneath the tree, and the slowly falling curtain, and the music, murmurous with destiny, that sings itself to sleep.

VI

"Siegfried"

I DO not compare the wines—I distinguish the qualities," remarked the delightful Dr. Middleton, shrewdest of fictional connoisseurs. And so, if fortune smiles upon the student of Wagner's scores, he learns, after a fashion, to distinguish (at least for his own uses) the qualities that set each of them in its place apart.

For each of Wagner's greater scores is, in some special way, uncompanioned. Where else in music is there anything like the blend of the idyllic and the tremendous that we find in *Siegfried?* When Wagner suspended work on the music of *Siegfried* after he had completed the composition-sketch as far as the end of Act II [1] and set out

[1] Wagner began the composition of *Siegfried* at Zürich, September 22, 1856. It was long supposed, on the basis of his letter of June 28, 1857, to Liszt, that when he stopped work on the music in that year he broke off before he had finished the composition of Act II. It is now definitely established by the researches of Dr. Otto Strobel in the Wagner archives at Bayreuth that Wagner in 1857 finished not only the composition-sketch of Act II, but the orchestral-sketch as well—the *Kompositionskizze* on July 30, the *Orchesterskizze* on August 9, 1857. Wagner resumed work on the orchestration of Act II at Munich, December 2, 1865: but again he was obliged to suspend work on the much-interrupted score. He completed the instrumentation of Act II

to rid himself, in *Tristan,* of the feverish ardors that were consuming him, he must have felt that even in its uncompleted form, even in the music of those first two Acts of the unfinished *Siegfried,* he had accomplished something for which he had not quite prepared us. This is music that on one page enchants us with its evocation of the beauty of the natural world; and, on another, awes us with the mysteriousness of the Sagas as the gray shadow of the Wanderer falls about us; and, on yet another, dilates us with the breath and daring of an epic world as Siegfried forges his recovered sword and holds it at last triumphantly aloft, while Wagner's music sweeps us through that jubilant fifty-five-bar cadence which is never noticed as a conquering feat of tonal structure only because it seems completely natural.

The power and titanic gusto of these pages were startling phenomena in the seventies. They are startling today. As we listen, the image of Siegfried the heroic and joyous youth grows and towers before our aural vision. For Wagner

at Triebschen, February 23, 1869. Within a week he had started the composition-sketch of Act III, the beginning of which is dated, so Dr. Strobel informs me, "March 1, 1869." The composition-sketch of Act III was finished on June 14, 1869, but the orchestral score was not completed until February 5, 1871. Wagner was therefore occupied intermittently with the music of *Siegfried* for more than fourteen years. The first performance was on August 16, 1876, at the first Bayreuth Festival.

possesses the ability to make us see with our ears. He is the supreme painter and dramatist among composers—as he is also the supreme musician— and can turn our hearing into vision when he wills. In these pages of *Siegfried* he brings to life for us the scene in that eventful smithy. We hear, and we see. When Siegfried plunges the hot metal into the water-trough, we seem to hear in the orchestra the steaming and hissing of the water. We see the white heat and the leaping flames of the forge, the gleaming of the formidable blade as Siegfried, his task concluded, brandishes "Nothung" aloft. But Wagner does not allow us to forget that the ultimate purpose of this tonal realism is something very different from mere musical delineation. Always, while the bellows groan and the hot steel sputters in the water and the sparks fly upward through Wagner's molten score, we are conscious of the greatness of the imaginative forces that are shaping the music. We become aware of some mysteriously creative property in the sunlit Spring woods outside the dark and noisome cave, and we realize that the life of a legendary world has been recaptured, and has overflowed into the music, filling it with that undrainable vitality and enchantment of which only Wagner knew the secret. The tone-painter and dramatist are companioned by a greater figure: Wagner the superb musician, the master of beautiful and renewing sound.

Tolstoi, in his heavy-handed way, made fun of the apparition of the Wanderer in the First Act of *Siegfried*—that inquisitorial visitor with his wide-brimmed hat and his "silly attitudes" (as Tolstoi thought them) who calls so inopportunely upon Mime. But what finally matters about the Wanderer in this scene is the image of him that is evoked by Wagner's music: those great chords for the brass that are the Wanderer's tonal incarnation. The "old, gray-bearded figure in his cloak colored like deep night, the terrible god that the old Scandinavians believed was wont to bestride the earth, who might enter at any moment their homesteads": a sorrowful, majestic figure, touched with the mystery and remoteness of the Sagas—this figure is realized in the music that Wagner wrote for him a thousand times more truthfully and completely than he could ever be through any combination of acting, make-up, costuming, or lighting.

In *Siegfried,* as habitually in his works, Wagner the alchemist turns everything into music. It is the invitation to make music that releases his imagination, and our own. Wagner the musician invariably prevails. He is better than his theories, better than his philosophy, better than his drama, essential as those are. For what seizes us and takes us captive, what we remember and return to with anticipation and delight, is the greatness of the music which this tone-poet has made the vehicle for all that he has to say to us. The musician touches scene or character or situation, a moment of prophecy or fulfillment, with his preternatural power, and we see life under a new aspect, in a new dimension, charged with a new beauty and significance.

Knowing his powers as he did, he relied upon his music to commend to us whatever he set upon his stage; and this reliance was well founded. The outward grotesquerie of the scene of Fafner's death, for example, did not tempt him to forget his obligation to pierce to the heart of the moment: and as Fafner begins to sing his death-song we hear in the orchestra a suggestion of that dolorous triplet figure with which Wagner was soon to do such memorable things in the second section of the Shepherd's melody in *Tristan*.

❀　　❀　　❀

But it is in the latter part of *Siegfried* that we confront the mightier Wagner. When he returned to his long-neglected score in afteryears, resuming his work on it in a joyous outburst of creative ardor such as he had seldom known, it was to fill the uncompleted portion, the sky-shouldering Third Act, with music of which the first two Acts had given us no hint. Such writing as this Act contains was new in Wagner, as it was new in music. The scene of the Wanderer's invocation of Erda in the storm-swept gorge, with its antique loftiness and grandeur, the scene of Brünnhilde's awakening, with its blinding radiance, its translation of luminosity into sound— these had no precedents in his works. The cloud-capped love duet that ends the Act is in another world from the high love-ritual of *Tristan,* it is in another world from anything that music had attempted.

"You must hear this last Act, the awakening of Brünnhilde," wrote Wagner to his old friend Pusinelli in January, 1870, from Triebschen. "My most beautiful thing! And I have also begun the *Götterdämmerung.* I must have much time, because whatever I write down is all superlative. But I'll still hold out, and then say to myself . . . 'Well, it's done, after all!' . . . So, out of everything, I derive new strength for life."

Elsewhere in the same letter he gives us a clear understanding of that "new strength for life" which, he says, he has derived; and he leaves us in no doubt of the fact that we should never have had the unapproachable products of his later years if it had not been for that nourishing serenity which his companionship with Cosima [2] had brought him.

"If my life thus far," he wrote, "has thrown me aimlessly through storms, then my life's ship, before it reached the haven, had to undergo the most extreme hardships. Nevertheless, the haven has been won. And now for the first time I may still live gladly and joyfully. A beautiful strong son, with high forehead and clear eye, Siegfried Richard, will inherit his father's name and preserve his works for the world. Forgive me for having observed a discreet silence in this matter about one who, as long as only assurances could speak for him, must await the time when the deed that clearly acknowledges his position will speak for him. This time is no longer far off [Wagner and Cosima were married in the following August] . . . Soon I shall have completed my fifty-seventh year of life, and I venture to perceive that it was just peace alone that I lacked in order to prove my strength when it was still in its purest effectiveness. Last summer, on that day when a

[2] Cosima, daughter of Franz Liszt and the Comtesse d'Agoult, was born at Bellagio, December 25, 1837. She married Hans von Bülow at Berlin, August 18, 1857. They were divorced, July 18, 1870, and Cosima married Wagner at Lucerne, August 25, 1870 (Wagner's first wife, Minna Planer, died at Dresden, January 25, 1866). Cosima Wagner died at Bayreuth, April 1, 1930, in her ninety-third year. She had outlived Wagner by almost half a century.

handsome son was born to more-than-happy me,[3]
I finished the [composition-sketch] of *Siegfried,*
which I had interrupted for eleven [*sic*] years.
An unheard-of thing! No one believed that I
would ever achieve it."

❧   ❧   ❧

Unheard-of indeed! Let us consider for a
moment what that task involved.

Wagner, as I have noted, began the music of
Siegfried at Zürich in September, 1856. He composed the First and Second Acts, and completed
the orchestral-sketch down to the end of Act II.
Then, in the Summer of 1857, he set the score
aside.

His negotiations with Breitkopf and Härtel
for the publication of the still-unfinished scores of
the *Ring* had fallen through. The consummation
of the formidable undertaking seemed for the

[3] Siegfried, son of Cosima and Richard, was born at Triebschen, June 6, 1869. The manuscript of the composition-sketch of
the last Act of *Siegfried* bears the inscription, in Wagner's hand:
"*Richtig Ausgetragen, 14 Juni 1869*"—eight days after the birth
of Wagner's son; and Cosima in her diary of June 13th says: "By
tomorrow he will probably have finished the sketch" [of the last
Act]. As the beginning of the manuscript of the composition-sketch
of this Act is inscribed by Wagner, "*1 März '69,*" it would appear
that he resumed work on the composition of *Siegfried* after an
interruption of almost twelve years, not "eleven," as he says in
the letter quoted above; for he had suspended his composition of
the music on July 30, 1857, after getting as far as the end of
Act II (see the note on p. 101). Wagner in his correspondence,
and also in his Autobiography, was sometimes careless in the
matter of dates.

108

present unattainable. Wagner felt the need of re-
newed contact with the stage and the public, the
need of immediate financial returns. Also, he had
fallen in love with his *Tristan* project—and with
Mathilde Wesendonck.

"Certain quite special considerations," he
wrote to ·Breitkopf and Härtel in September,
1857, "have caused me to break off my work upon
the *Nibelungs* for a while in order to carry out at
once a subject which I conceived some years
previously. A chief consideration was my wish to
take in hand a work that, being far less exacting
in performance, would afford me the possibility
of actually producing it immediately upon completion [4] . . . I determined to interrupt my
greater work [the *Ring*], and am now on the
point of beginning the musical composition of my
previously completed poem of *Tristan und Isolde*
—for such is to be the name of my work . . ."

So Wagner put aside Siegfried and Mime
and the Wanderer and the Forest Bird, and flung
himself, instead of his audacious Siegfried, into
the fires that blazed between himself and his desire—that ungovernable desire which, at the moment, was a composite of *Tristan* and Mathilde.

Thereafter began that long period of

[4] Wagner was disappointed in this, as in so many other
matters at that time: *Tristan* had to wait almost six years after
its completion before it reached the stage.

enormous effort and distraction which lay between the temporary abandonment of *Siegfried*
in 1857 and the composition of its final Act in
1869. Consider the astonishing record of those
crowded years that intervened between the day
when Wagner left Siegfried to his own devices
and the day when at last he led his hero into
Brünnhilde's reluctantly eager arms. Between
1857 and 1869, Wagner wrote the poem and
music of *Tristan;* recomposed the first two scenes
of *Tannhäuser;* wrote *Die Meistersinger;* worked
on the *Parsifal* drama; saw *Tannhäuser, Tristan,*
and *Die Meistersinger* put on the stage; con-
certized in various cities of Europe; published
the *Nibelungen* poem; [5] released a stream of arti-
cles, essays, pamphlets; won the heart and patron-
age of a King and the devotion of a great woman.
Then, a dozen years after he had left them, he
reëntered those ancient, silent woods where Siegfried and the Forest Bird had been transfixed so
long before, disenchanted them, and brought the
hero through Brünnhilde's flames.

No wonder he himself considered that he had
pulled off something of a feat by this reorienta-
tion of his mind and spirit in that receding
world of the imagination from which they had
been exiled by his own decree—this long-delayed
return from the linden-scented, moonlit streets of

[5] It had been issued privately in 1853.

homespun Nuremberg to the epic world of the Sagas; from Hans Sachs to the Wanderer: truly an immeasurable distance!

❦ ❦ ❦

Wagner's nature and activities made it difficult for him to be entirely free from the agitating currents of the outer world. He was a natural storm-centre, and he remained so through most of his existence, a source and victim of more or less continuous turmoil. Yet that freedom to "live gladly and joyfully" of which he spoke in the letter of 1870 from which I have quoted, that serenity and inner peace, that profound appeasement of the spirit which he derived from Cosima's companionship, provided a rich and inexhaustible soil for the creative abundance of those wonderful years that began at Triebschen in 1866 with the resumption of *Die Meistersinger,* continued there and at Bayreuth with Act III of *Siegfried* and with *Götterdämmerung* and *Parsifal,* and ended at Venice in 1883 only with the breaking of the iron will and the stopping of the giant heart and the closing of the visionary eyes.

Wagner and Cosima von Bülow, seeking refuge in Switzerland, had discovered Triebschen on the last day of March, 1866, while taking a trip on the Lake of Lucerne. They found "a simple little two-storied house rising on a project-

ing tongue of land in peaceful, parklike surround-
ings, among venerable trees," as Cosima described it in her diary. One can see this wooded
peninsula from the promenade that runs along the
lake before the Kurhaus and the Hotel Nationale,
at Lucerne; and from one's balcony on the front
of that excellent hostelry one can almost discern,
among the trees a mile across the water, the house
whence issued such abounding wealth.

On Easter Sunday of 1866 Richard and
Cosima inspected the villa, and Wagner saw with
delight that he had found what he wanted. He at
once rented the property for a year (he remained
there for six)—"nobody," he declared, "will get
me out of here again." On May 12th, Cosima,
with her children, left Munich and joined him at
Triebschen (she was in Munich during part of
1867 and 1868, but rejoined Wagner at Triebschen in the latter year, and remained with him
thenceforth).

Their life at Triebschen was idyllic. "We
live here as though in a fairy-tale," wrote Cosima
to King Ludwig . . . "About midday, our Friend
[Wagner] tells me what he has done during the
morning. In the afternoon he roams about the
pastures and meadows, and I usually go to meet
him. He then spends a little time with me and the
children, who are very happy here. In the evening
he dictates to me his autobiography . . . He is

just hailing me in the distance; am I not right in saying that we are living in a fairy-tale, and have found sweet forgetfulness of life? We hear nothing but the tinkle of bells as the herds of cattle descend from the high pastures and wander in the meadows which have been cleared among the woods, gazing at us every day in friendly curiosity with their great eyes . . . A strangely happy dream."

It is heartening to realize that the person who most truly appreciated Wagner was the remarkable woman who dwelt with him in his later years, sustaining him during that period when he needed most the help that she could give him. No one can read the deeply affecting and revealing excerpts from her letters and diary without, I think, becoming convinced that the latter part of Wagner's career would have been a tragically different thing if Cosima had not thrown in her lot with his.

The story of Cosima's life with Wagner is the story of a self-abnegation unexampled in the history of great geniuses, not only for its completeness, but for the magnitude of its results: for Cosima's unselfishness was not, as unselfishness so often is, sterile and negative, but rich in imaginative and intellectual fruitfulness.

She was irradiated by Wagner's mind. Nothing that he offered her taxed her capacity for assimilation. And for her, he was not only a great genius, but a great man. Knowing well his personal history and his failings (for she was a penetrating and a just assessor of character), she could still say of him, "Whoever is used to his company, whoever has known his spirit and his mind, must remain indifferent to everyone else."

That this conviction was in some degree a triumph of belief over trial is made evident on many pages of Cosima's frank and intimate confessions. The Master was never easy to live with; and there are few things more touching in the Diary than those passages which reveal to us the limitless tact, the limitless patience, the limitless devotion and self-sacrifice, with which Cosima solved the problem of being Richard Wagner's helpmate.

She dwelt with the uncertainly amiable Richard for almost two decades, enduring not only the criticism of society, but suffering recurrently the harsh tongue and the difficult humors of the terrible Titan whom she had chosen to live with and to cherish. She did little else but serve him. Not only did she bear him children when it was opprobrious to do so, but she stood between him and the world, in order that that world might be immeasurably enriched. She knew what sort of letter to write on behalf of Wagner to a half-mad King, and what sort of letter would best suit a former inamorata. She knew how to deal with publishers and artists and creditors and importunate intruders. She could discuss Greek tragedy with the Titan as competently as she could order the Titan's meals and keep the children out of earshot. She knew that she was living with a preeminent genius, and that her first duty was to see that nothing interfered with the output of that unparalleled brain. So far as she could help it, nothing did.

It is pleasant to imagine the happiness and comfort that Cosima wove above Wagner in that secluded dwelling on the Lake of Lucerne where so many treasures of the mind were brought forth. In one of her letters to the young King who had lifted Wagner from the depths of despair, she has left us a communicative picture of the Triebschen house (now converted into a Wagner Museum) : "On the wall of the drawing-room hang the *Tannhäuser* picture and the *Rheingold* drawings in all their glory; and the busts of the guardian spirit of this home and of the Spirit whom he protects, lend it a finish. Opposite the long wall, in a well-lighted position between the two doors, hangs the portrait in oils, the first birthday present, beneath which are amassed all the gorgeous things received in the course of his life by our Friend. There are silver goblets and wreaths, in the midst of which stand out splendidly the two statues of Tannhäuser and Lohengrin. Between the two windows stands the piano, over which hang the medallions of Liszt and Bülow. The little room next the drawing-room has become the library. It is extraordinarily quiet and comfortable downstairs here. Upstairs is the work-room. . . . Our Friend is just coming to table, to dine and seek recreation among the children. Russ, the gigantic dog, who is impossible to train, and Kos, the badly trained terrier, also add to the snug atmosphere; and the two peacocks, Wotan and Frigga, strut proudly and tranquilly about the garden. . . . Just now, the library was turned into a nursery. Our Friend first played with the children, then sat down at the piano and went through some of the Ninth Symphony. While at one and the same time I was drawing into my soul the glorious strains, enjoying the quiet merriment of the children, and sharing our Friend's sense of well-being, I could not help thinking of you with tears of emotion. It is you who have conjured up this rich world of peace amid one of agony, it is you who have made it possible for us to be together: it is you who have given peace to the mind which never knew it before."

Many hard things have been said of Wagner the man, and some of them are probably true. But it is important to remember, as we look back upon the history of a genius whose debt to him the world can never liquidate, that for Cosima, the woman who knew him best, who was acutely and sorrowfully aware of all his faults, Wagner the human being was worthy not only of her love, but of her adoration.

"I should like," she wrote in her diary for none but her children to see, "to give the children the clearest possible idea of Wagner's nature. But I feel that the attempt is a failure. How am I to reproduce the sound of his voice, the quality of his charm? Yet, perhaps, these words are better than nothing, and so I go blundering on." She was deeply moved by Carlyle's eulogy of Goethe, because it applied, she said, "so absolutely to Richard—to his genuineness, his sincerity, his courage, his goodness."

Conscious of his every failing, having suffered grievously from his wounding ways, Cosima could still say of Wagner that she was "overwhelmed by his goodness" to her; could still call him the revealer "of all that was noble and true."

Wagner could have paid her a similar tribute; for he worshipped her—as well he might have. And the memory of Cosima, the consort of Richard Wagner, should be cherished by all who value the contributions of Wagner's genius to the art of the world. For had it not been for Cosima's penetrating comprehension, her inflexible will, her complete selflessness, her inveterate sympathy, her practical aid, the world, in all likelihood, would not now possess *Die Meistersinger, Siegfried, Götterdämmerung,* and *Parsifal,* those works of Wagner's later years which crowned his superhuman labors.

In those inexhaustibly fruitful days at Triebschen, Wagner lived with an unhampered expressiveness and felicity and contentment which he had never known. He and Cosima read together Sophocles, Shakespeare, Goethe, Cervantes. They played Haydn symphonies four-hand, or Wagner played Bach chorales for Cosima. ("See," he remarked to her, "with what equanimity Bach writes the boldest, most audacious things.") But those hours were richest for them both when he played her his own music, passages from works in hand: in 1866-67, *Die Meistersinger;* in 1869-70, the Third Act of *Siegfried;* then and later, *Götterdämmerung.* When he played even such familiar matter as the *Tristan* Prelude, she could scarcely preserve her self-control. "At such moments," she wrote afterward, "all I know is that, in Elsa's words, 'for thee would I go to meet death.'" As she stood in her lakeside garden, her thoughts were long: "I was enraptured by the snow-covered mountains in their mysterious, ever-lasting, motionless dance; and I became sud-

denly aware of the music through which exalted
natures reflect themselves for us in sound. I felt
the transience of all personal existence. The
eternal essence of all greatness rises, a radiant
message, from the pale mirror of the lake."

Wagner resorted often to the heights near
Triebschen for the silence and solitude which his
spirit needed as he worked upon the greater pages
of the *Ring*. "Those mountain peaks," wrote
Cosima, "belonged to the world in which he conceived his scores, and to which he often returned
for strength to carry them on." For Wagner, like
other masters of life, went up into the hills for
creative renewal. Often, in the flesh, he and
Cosima ascended the mountains near Lucerne,
and waited for the dawn in the clear sharp air;
and Wagner, like Nietzsche's Zarathustra, learned
wisdom from the beauty and divinity of the sky
and earth and light, and returned to his study in
Triebschen to work upon the final Act of *Siegfried*.

It is astonishing how seldom one finds it
necessary to remind oneself that in the total *Siegfried* we are dealing with a score of heterogeneous
texture. Yet *Siegfried,* like *Tannhäuser,* is a work
that represents two different periods of Wagner's
development. When he began work on the music
of *Siegfried* (six months after he had finished

the scoring of *Die Walküre*), he was in his forty-fourth year; when he rose from the instrumentation of the completed work, he was fifty-eight. For almost fifteen years, therefore, *Siegfried* had been in his desk; and into the middle of the gap that divided the score had intruded such disturbing aliens as Tristan and Isolde, Venus, Tannhäuser, Leda and her Swan, Europa and her Bull, and the Mastersingers of Nuremberg. Is it not remarkable that the score exhibits the continuity that it does—that only the prying student can tell the difference between the product of 1856-57 and the product of 1869-71?

For Wagner the sovereign artist has found a way to integrate the later *Siegfried* with the earlier. He himself was aware of his ability "to mediate and knit together," as he once expressed it: his mastery of what he liked to call "the art of transition"; and he has accomplished with superlative mastery the addition of his later *Siegfried* Act to those that preceded it in time and style; so that we scarcely realize, until we set about the work of comparative musical anatomy, that the Third Act of *Siegfried* is the product of a subtler musical mind, a craftier and more resourceful musical technique, than the two earlier Acts. The Wagner who wrote Act III of *Siegfried* had behind him *Tristan und Isolde* and *Die Meistersinger* and the music of the Paris Venus-

berg. He had learned from *Tristan* a good deal
more about the possibilities of harmonic speech
than he had known when he dreamed of Siegfried
in Mime's cave and Fafner's woods. He had
learned both from *Tristan* and from *Die Meistersinger* what can be wrought by a daring master
of polyphonic art.

Turn to the music that accompanies Siegfried's words, "Ach! wie schön! Schimmernde
Wolken," as the hero, removing the helmet of the
sleeper underneath the fir-tree on the mountain
height, gazes on the quiet figure with its shining,
unloosed hair. Note the delicate adroitness with
which Wagner handles that exquisite shifting of
ninth-chords between the keys of B major and
E. It is only a transition from dominant to tonic;
but with what finesse and craft it is accomplished
by the aid of that magically suspended D-
sharp of the clarinet! There is nothing like this in
the earlier portion of the score. As he proceeds
with the final Act of *Siegfried,* these subtleties
of harmonic texture become more frequent. He
can set that utterance of Brünnhilde's sorrowful brooding, "Ich sehe der Brünne prangenden
Stahl," and find a new way to voice regret and
the sense of loss. That reiterated triplet figure in
thirty-second-notes for the strings has a *Götterdämmerung* flavor—as we shall realize later when
we find it again in the Second Act of that tragedy.

What is still more remarkable, it has, a few bars later in the *Siegfried* passage, a quality that we shall scarcely find again until we reach *Parsifal* and the end of Wagner's long, eventful road.

And what a lordly polyphonist he has become! Turn back to the orchestral passage that accompanies Siegfried's advance through Loge's flames, and note with how superb an ease and how superb a beauty the master weaves his gorgeous instrumental tapestry out of five great themes. There is no such triumphant ease of handling and fertility of resource in the earlier pages of the *Ring*.

There are many treasures in the two first Acts of *Siegfried;* but not until we reach the final Act, with its strangely blended amplitude and subtlety of style, do we realize how far we have come on the path of Wagner's conquering advance.

❁   ❁   ❁

In the orchestral introduction to this Act, the doomed Wanderer upon an earth about to be reborn seeks counsel of Erda the Sibyl in the stormy dusk. This music, of topless grandeur, is filled with a sense of the encompassing terror and mysteriousness of Nature, of those secrets of wisdom and destiny, death and restoration, with which the depths are charged; so that the visit of the Wanderer to Erda the seeress, gleaming with hoarfrost in the mountain night, becomes that eminence on Wagner's complex and vast terrain whence we perceive that the universe is well designed.

Later, the music of this Act is swept with the roar of legendary flames and winds and is luminous with a supermundane splendor. Wagner was in his late fifties when he composed the scene of Brünnhilde's awakening, with its prodigious evocation of the dawn. Yet, as we listen to this music, our vision of its creator, of the small and tired man, worn with strife and passion and unimaginable toil,—already afflicted with symptoms of the heart disease that eventually killed him,— becomes gigantic like the work itself, "the appearance of a god coming over it." His own creation, Siegfried the Lifegiver, seems to have restored to him that superhuman power of which *Siegfried* the music-drama was the issue; and this music, afire with procreative ardor and immortal strength, assumes its place among the seven wonders of the creative mind.

Wagner seems to have found a kind of physical rejuvenation in the mere process of completing the inordinate work. This is the tonal speech of an exuberant Titan. No other music that Wagner wrote has quite this cloud-bestriding ecstasy, this conquering and jocund strength. Cosima rejoiced in the sight of him as he sat at the piano, playing and singing for her certain passages from the final scene as he composed them. "What delights me most of all," she wrote, "is the look in his face as he sits opposite me; his eye grows dark and flashes, and his resonant voice shakes me inexpressibly."

It was the music especially of the final scene that stirred them both; and Cosima records in her diary that she said to Wagner: "This awakening of love in the young Siegfried, who has no idea of woman or of what a woman is, who is exalted and fortified by this woman who has already sat before the book of life and is so much wiser than he—this, and your music for it, seem to me unique." And Wagner responded gaily: "Yes, I can still compose!"

He was happy, indeed, over the whole tremendous Act. Certainly, these pages stand alone for sheer resplendence and prodigal gloriousness of beauty. This music, like an emanation of light, for the first time makes radiance an experience of the ear. And this is not chiefly a matter of dazzling investiture, but of the music's actual creative substance. The musical thought itself, the imaginative texture, is supremely great.

❦   ❦   ❦

These patterns of excessive beauty, these sounds and winds and echoes from Wagner's

mountain of the gods, pose a formidable problem
for the singing-actress who would realize for us
the Brünnhilde of this climactic scene. Yet many
of those who have heard the *Siegfried* Brünnhilde
of Kirsten Flagstad must have felt that this was
the Brünnhilde of *Siegfried* as Wagner intended
and created her—that thus would she have looked
and spoken, risen and stood, exulted and feared
and loved.

From the moment that she waked and rose
upon her couch and looked about her, raising her
arms in greeting to the sun, the light, the day, accompanied by music whose resurrectional ecstasy
transforms the world, she was the visual and
aural image of Wagner's tonal poetry. The beauty
and fidelity of the offered image—the gestures of
touching simplicity, dignity, naturalness, and
grace, the lustrous purity of the voice: these were
living symbols of the majesty and tenderness of
Wagner's creative thought.

The use of the voice, the delivery of the
musical phrases and the words, were ceaselessly
expressive. When she sang, "Lang war mein
Schlaf," the sadness that clouded momentarily the
shining tones was like a passing memory of the
Valkyr's tragic punishment. But the lofty and
heroic splendor with which she shaped the con-
tours of her greeting to the gods and to the morn-

ing earth were fretted with the golden fire of Wagner's mountain dawn.

Her whole awakening scene, from the moment when she greets with inevitable gestures the recovered light of heaven and the sweet security of earth, to the transporting moment when she joins her voice with Siegfried's, is like a tonal epitome of Shelley's hymning of the morning sun in passage after passage of *Prometheus Unbound*.

Hearing Brünnhilde's "Heil dir, leuchtender Tag!" where the rapturous voice is lifted above the soaring thirds of the exulting orchestra, we feel that music such as this must have come from sources deeper than the temporal self—that it must incarnate some inner and immortal dayspring of the spirit. For a luminous interval we find ourselves miraculously released and quickened, reborn and weariless. "The morning wind blows again . . . Olympus is but the outside of the earth." We forget that we were ever captive, and know that we are free.

VII

"Götterdämmerung"

IN THE year that Brahms completed his First
Symphony and Saint-Saëns worked upon
Samson et Dalila and the American people celebrated their first century of independence, a
musical lunatic of genius issued to the world a
preposterous invitation. He bade them visit an
unattractive and uncomfortable theatre (that
"madman's folly," as he himself called it) which
he had built in a remote, provincial German town,
where the lodgings were primitive, the food a
gamble, the prices high. He asked them to sit
in a totally darkened auditorium, on penitential
wooden seats, and follow in quiet the slow progress of a gigantic four-part musical drama lasting some fourteen hours in actual performance,
and traversing four days. Amazingly enough, the
most distinguished public that had ever gathered
for an operatic première flocked to witness the
unheard-of exhibition—emperors and kings and
princes and diplomats and artists and musicians
and critics from the ends of the earth; and, after
it was all over, there were some among them who
realized that the impossible lunatic who had de-

vised it was the creator of a new and epoch-making art.

Opera-going had for centuries been a pastime, at which the boxholders played cards or ate ices when they were bored. Wagner turned it into a religion of beauty and philosophy. Operatic audiences had always enjoyed the excitement of interrupting a performance with applause and encores. Wagner prohibited applause, and made encores inconceivable. He taught an international public how to listen to great music—in silence and with respect. He made over the mental and social habits of opera-goers throughout the world, so that today we take it as a matter of course that a great work of musico-dramatic art demands acceptance as one of the loftiest and most exalting of all experiences, as it was with the ancient Greeks. In our time, in the foremost lyric theatres of every nation that retains a culture, this feat of artistic and social regeneration is unconsciously commemorated whenever Wagner's *Ring* is given at festival performances.

🏵 🏵 🏵

Those who reflect upon the things they witness, and know something of the history and significance of what is set before them, must often draw their breath a little faster as they come to the end of *Götterdämmerung*. They will remember that this stupendous *Ring* of Wagner's, which touches all heights, all depths, and all immensities, was planned and accomplished by one man over a period of more than a quarter of a century. The whole of its dramatic and poetic structure and almost three-fourths of its music (*Rheingold, Die Walküre,* and the first two Acts of *Siegfried*) were completed virtually without encouragement or help, by a man who was usually poor and often ill, and for more than a dozen years an exile.[1] When Wagner laid its foundations in November, 1848, he was thirty-five years old, and had just completed *Lohengrin.* When he set down the last note of the orchestral score of *Götterdämmerung,* on November 21, 1874 [2]—twenty-six years almost to a day from the time when he began what was to be the *Ring*—he was sixty-one, had completed

[1] Wagner, exiled from Germany for complicity in the Dresden uprising of 1849, was amnestied (except in Saxony) in 1860. In 1862, a final amnesty permitted his return to Saxony as well as to the rest of Germany.

[2] He worked upon the music of *Götterdämmerung* over a period of a little more than five years and a month. He began the composition-sketch (with the Norn scene, not with the brief orchestral Vorspiel), October 2, 1869. The composition-sketch of Act III was finished on April 10, 1872, and the orchestral score on November 21, 1874. The first performance was at Bayreuth, August 17, 1876. From Dr. Otto Strobel, curator of the archives at Wahnfried, one learns that Wagner's musical manuscripts of the *Ring* comprise no fewer than 3,000 pages of orchestral scoring. Those composers who know what it means to write out one page of orchestral scoring may be able to form some dim idea of Wagner's prodigious labors—and he composed a dozen other operatic scores.

all his works save *Parsifal,* and had surmounted difficulties and ordeals that would have broken a will less steel-like than his own.

It is illuminating to know that in the Summer and Autumn of 1874, at Bayreuth, although Cosima was aware of the profound inner agitation that possessed him as he neared his goal,—the scoring of that apocalyptic finale with its "blazing up of eternity like a flame,"—Wagner remained incorrigibly cheerful, and found diversion in, of all things, Boïeldieu's *Dame blanche* and Xenophon's *Anabasis!* When the end was accomplished, and the last note of the score of *Götterdämmerung* and the completed *Ring* was set down, he realized that he had achieved a thing without a parallel. But he had always known that he would achieve it: his faith in his powers and predestination never wavered.

As usual, his faith was justified superbly by the outcome. There is no such example of sustained and vitalized creative thinking as the *Ring* in music or in any other art. This vast projection of the creative vision and the preponent will: this four-part epic in drama and in tones whose progress unfolds a cosmic parable of nature and destiny and gods and demigods and men; which begins in the ancient river's depths and ends in the flaming heavens that consume Valhalla's deities and bring the promise of a new day of enlightened generosity and reconciliatory love—this was a work without precedent or pattern. No one before had dreamt of creating a dramatic symphony lasting fourteen hours, organized and integrated and coherent. Only a fanatically daring brain and imagination, only a lunatic of genius, could have projected such a thing; only a superman could have accomplished it.

There is nothing that can be set beside it, nothing that yields to the imagination so moving and eventful a retrospect as the close of *Götterdämmerung,* that soaring peak whence we look backward over the long way we came, and see again in memory those unforgettable happenings that were to follow Wotan's primal sin. Only Wagner could have built from the dark, unplumable depths of Alberich's cupidity and hate, upward across the gulfs and hills and worlds and heavens of the *Ring's* ungirdled universe, into the light of Brünnhilde's selfless and heroic and sacrificial love, where we are "lifted into the great mood and touched with the undying"; so that we are left, at the end, with our inveterate wonder at this boundless imagination which could hold all nature and all humanity in the secret depths of its creative will.

❀   ❀   ❀

In *Götterdämmerung* we face the loftiest peak of that singular and towering range, "the gigantic mountain-chain of the *Ring*," as Liszt called it, the like of which no summoning will but Wagner's could have flung against the startled sky. Of all his utterances, this is the one that is couched most prevailingly and influentially in the grand style. It is not the most lovable of his scores, nor the most symmetrical in form, nor the most consistent in its texture. But it is beyond comparison the most tremendous. To speak of *Götterdämmerung* as "Aeschylean" is to be over-flattering to Greece. The tragic grandeur, the sweep and weight and impact of the colossal work, are almost crushing to imperfectly insulated temperaments. It is a lonely and unpredicted apparition, and one may doubt if anyone now living will ever see its equal.

Time after time in the great septet of scores that came from him in his maturity, Wagner compassed the sublime; and three at least of these instances occur in the final drama of the *Ring*. They are, of course, Waltraute's narrative, Siegfried's death and the funeral hymn [3] that follows, and Brünnhilde's self-immolation. These are the pinnacles of the work. But always we are aware of

[3] Wagner himself characterized the *Götterdämmerung* Trauer-musik as a "chorus which is, as it were, sung by the orchestra after Siegfried's death during the change of scene."

the might of *Götterdämmerung:* of the stature and the stride of its participants, and the distant, watching gods. Yet these immensities are threaded with some of the loveliest music that Wagner ever wrote. Even as Waltraute draws herself level with the divine sorrow of "Dann noch einmal, zum letzten Mal," our ears are still retaining the quiet ecstasy of Brünnhilde's "An meiner Wonne willst du dich weiden?"

The immortal Joseph Bennett complained in the unregenerate old days that one of the troubles with *Götterdämmerung* is that "it has so few themes that had not previously been heard in the other dramas of the *Ring*"; "there are only thirteen," he remarked plaintively, "as against thirty-five in *Rheingold,* twenty-two in *Walküre,* twenty in *Siegfried* [*sic*]." Concerning which one might remark that the innocent Mr. Bennett could have inspired Rodin's comment on another matter: "He should have looked again." But even if it were true that Wagner had introduced only thirteen new themes into the score of *Götterdämmerung,* we should still have to praise him for their consummate expressiveness, the eloquence with which they utter what Wagner intended them to say. And we should also have to praise him for the baffling art with which he has contrived to surround and penetrate them with the same imaginative and characterizing quality: a

quality indigenous to the spirit of this drama—
that sense of an ominous, threatening, storm-shot
sky which seems to brood above it.

The music of *Götterdämmerung* is taut and
surcharged in a way that is peculiar to itself.
Throughout the whole of the wide-ranging score
we are conscious of the note of an impending
doom, of a vague and cumulative dread. With the
pianissimo chord of the minor ninth for the wood
and tubas and arpeggiated muted strings that falls
upon the music like a mysterious hand as the curtains open on the shrouded mystery of the Norn
scene, this sense of ineluctable catastrophe is
established by the music, and is maintained almost unbrokenly throughout the work.

But that suggestion of inescapable catastrophe is only part, and not the greater part, of
what Wagner meant to say to us in *Götterdämmerung*. Its true significance is in its overtones
and implications.

Wagner was a spiritual mystic, and neither
his dramas nor his music are wholly comprehen-
sible to the student or listener who is unfamiliar
with the philosophical backgrounds against which
Wagner set his parables of the spiritual life. During the last two years that he worked on the music
of *Götterdämmerung,* he and Cosima steeped
themselves in the mystical literature of the ancient
Hindus, "finding in it not only themselves, but

also the great conceptions that guided Wagner as a man and a creative artist"; and as late as 1872 Wagner had apparently intended to retain certain mystical utterances in one of the several versions of Brünnhilde's final oration, which he ultimately discarded. In a remarkable passage of that vale-dictory, Brünnhilde proclaims herself a being enlightened by sorrowing love, about to attain the blessed state of liberation from rebirth. Cosima, as she records in her diary, was not satisfied with some of Wagner's phrases; so he dropped the passage and shortened the close.

Probably the omitted words would not have been comprehended except by those who, like Wagner himself, were students of Hindu philosophy. But though the words that Brünnhilde sings, in Wagner's final version of the close of *Götterdämmerung,* have nothing to say to us of enlightening and redemptive love, Wagner's music, in the orchestral postlude that follows the Immolation scene, tells us only and finally of that.

Brünnhilde has sung the matchless valedictory, overwhelming in its utterance of grief and reproach and prophecy and lofty dedication, that is the dramatic and musical culmination of the *Ring*. It is also an implied foreshadowing of the new order, the new day of equity and love, that will succeed the twilight of the gods and the night of their destruction. We glean from Brünnhilde's soliloquy that she perceives the divine justice of self-sacrifice. Her vision is that of a seeress discerning a regenerate world, and she prepares to join her dead hero on the funeral pyre in order that she may fulfill the last necessity which shall make that vision a reality—though all this is implicit in the music rather than explicit in the words. She has drawn the Ring from Siegfried's finger, and put it on her own, to be recovered from her ashes by the waiting River and the Rhine Daughters, who will cherish forever the cleansed and purified gold. She turns toward the back, where Siegfried's body has already been laid upon the flower-strewn pyre. She seizes a great firebrand from one of the staring vassals, and hurls it among the logs, which break into sudden flame. Two young men bring forward Grane her horse. She goes to it, quickly unbridles it, bends to it affectionately, addresses it. In rising ecstasy, she cries aloud their joint greeting to the dead Siegfried, swings herself onto Grane's back, and together they leap into the flames.

The fire blazes up, filling the whole space before the hall, as the terrified men and women crowd toward the back. The Rhine overflows, and the Rhine Daughters are seen swimming forward. Hagen plunges into the flood, and is drawn beneath the surface by two of the maidens as Alberich's Curse motive is thundered in his unheeding ears, while Flosshilde exultantly holds on high the recovered Ring. As the hall collapses in ruins, an increasing glow in the heavens reveals Valhalla, the gods and heroes seated within, awaiting majestically their doom. Flames seize upon the castle of those who were once so mighty and so ruthless and so proud; while in the orchestra, high on the violins and flute, a final transfigured repetition of the motive of Redeeming Love soars above the wreckage of autocracy and power and the selfish pride of gods.

❦ ❦ ❦

Thus the work ends upon the note of lofty reconciliation and spiritual assuagement that is characteristic of Wagner's practice as a master of poetic tragedy. For he never lets us forget the transforming and clarifying backgrounds against which his greater tragedies are played. The scene of Brünnhilde's immolation is the thing of wonder it remains because its tragic pathos is seen in the light of a mysteriously solacing appeasement. The sublimity of her farewell to the doomed Wotan, "Ruhe, ruhe, du Gott!" gives us an abiding sense of that high intuition of human destiny which Wagner always knew how to suggest to us in his music; so that we are reminded, at the last, that "if a man will consider life in its whole circuit, and see how superabundantly it is furnished with what is extraordinary and beautiful and great, he shall soon know for what we were born."

Wagner, an insatiable student of all Eastern thought and art, might almost have remembered the curiously similar passage which closes the *Salámán and Absál* of the Sufi poet Jámi, who, like Wagner, used the parable of an exalting love as a touchstone of mystical enlightenment in his fifteenth-century poem, with its final words that Wagner's Brünnhilde would have understood:

> . . . So now
> Of sere wood strewn about the plain of Death,
> A raft to bear them through the wave of Fire
> Into annihilation he devis'd,
> Gather'd, and built; and, firing with a torch,
> Into the central flame Absal and he
> Sprung hand in hand, exulting. But the sage
> In secret all had order'd; and the flame,
> Directed by his self-fulfilling will,
> Devouring Her to ashes, left untouch'd
> Salaman—all the baser metal burn'd,
> And to itself the authentic Gold return'd.

❀   ❀   ❀

To perform *Götterdämmerung,* or to impersonate any one of its major characters, without conveying at least some hint of the pregnant quality of the work, is to commit one of those acts of aesthetic betrayal which great masterpieces are so often called upon to suffer. A Brünnhilde, a Siegfried, a Waltraute, untouched by a sense of the music-drama's tension, would be travesties like unto a frigid Isolde or an Apollonian Mime: for always in the music of *Götterdämmerung* the sensitive ear detects that note of impending crisis and inescapable disaster to which I have referred. Beddoes might have been thinking of *Götterdämmerung* (if it had been composed and he had known it) when he heard those distant, terrible, heart-shaking rumors, and cried that

> ". . . Time into Eternity
> Falls over ruined worlds."

An untensed *Götterdämmerung* is as preposterous (alas, it is not unthinkable!) as a pulseless *Tristan*. Even the tonal sunlight that plays upon some of the more exultant music of the score—the auroral pages of the love duo, the brilliant noontide of the Rhine Journey, Siegfried's narrative—is shadowed, here and there, with the advancing grayness of a sombre dusk.

It is because the leading characters in *Götterdämmerung* must keep themselves harmoniously and vibrantly alive to all these things—the tension of the play and music, the greatness of the work's essential style, its overtones of high and luminous intuition—that its problems tower mountain-high for its interpreters.

The fabulous Lilli Lehmann once declared that the three Brünnhildes were relatively easy to interpret because "you are so carried away by the dramatic emotion, the action, and the scene, that you do not have to think of how to sing. . . . That comes of itself." Perhaps it did, for Lilli. But with due respect for the opinion of the amaranthine artist who first revealed the *Götterdämmerung* Brünnhilde to New York,[4] a complete dramatic and musical revelation of anyone of the three Brünnhildes probably remains, for most opera-goers of today, the ultimate test of a dramatic soprano.

This is especially true of the task set for the interpreter who would achieve an imaginative re-creation of the heroine whose greatness of love, greatness of anguish, and greatness of exaltation form the basic theme of *Götterdämmerung*—a task that might well dismay an artist gifted with merely human powers.

The mightiest crescendo posed for a dramatic soprano is that which is represented by the growth of Brünnhilde from the heroically loving woman of the *Götterdämmerung* Prologue to the sublimated prophetess of the Finale, with her lofty grief and her encompassing wisdom. It is Kirsten Flagstad's prime achievement that she makes real for us this progress and culmination. She is able,

[4] On January 25, 1888, at the Metropolitan Opera House.

140

at the close, to leave us face to face with that great figure of Wagner's imagination which comes to full stature at the drama's end, when Brünnhilde, the transfigured seeress, no longer wholly of this world, enters with tranquil majesty upon the drama's final scene of tragic horror and recrimination, and (as though Wagner had remembered the Euripidean line) "holds a hand uplifted over hate." When she sings of "Siegfrieds Liebe" in the scene with Waltraute, the color of the tones, the sound of the syllables, are the ultimate voicing of blissful serenity and faith. But later, in the Immolation scene, she can drench with fathomless sorrow her disclosure of what she had come to know of that "treueste Liebe" which the beloved one could betray; and in the semitonal fall of the voice on "Liebe" she makes us feel the anguish of Brünnhilde's piteous comprehension.

Only the *Götterdämmerung* Brünnhilde has such music to sing as those gloriously free-winged and soaring and enraptured phrases in the duet with Siegfried in the Prologue, and in her scene with Waltraute, which utter the beatitude of her love; and only Kirsten Flagstad, in the experience of this generation, has sung them with so lofty an ecstasy and tenderness. "So zur Seligsten schuf mich die Strafe," sings Brünnhilde; and afterward, in that wondrous E-flat cantilena which is one of the transporting moments of all music, her exalted passion bears her far above the treacherous world.

Mme. Flagstad sets before us a Brünnhilde achieving tragic growth and exaltation by a process of spiritual intensification as secret and interior as it is unfailingly indicative. By the subtlest of changes in expression; by the aid of that eloquent repose and that reticent art of miming which she has mastered; above all, by the beauty and intensity of her singing, she reveals Brünnhilde's spirit, moulding astonishingly the flesh. The outer image is lighted from within, becomes translucent and transformed. One recalls nothing more exact in its imaginative veracity than the attitude and gestures of this Brünnhilde as she sits among the falling shadows of her mountaintop, kissing Siegfried's ring, awaiting the return of the hero who is shortly to betray her: nothing more piercing in its fidelity than the indescribable gesture—overwhelming in its compassionate tenderness—with which, at the tragedy's end, she removes that selfsame ring from the finger of the dead Siegfried who once had torn it from her own.

Mme. Flagstad's delivery of the subduing peroration is extraordinary for its loftiness of mood and its transilluminated beauty. It is filled with the essential quality of Brünnhilde's valedictory; with that noble grieving, that depth of sorrowful reproach, that exalted and expiatory transport, which make this farewell to earth and earthly love and all felicity the most wonderful thing of its kind in the world's art, beside which every other leave-taking in drama or poetry or music seems relatively earth-bound and limited.

From the tragedy's beginning to its end she is its nobly projected image, growing, as it grows, in poignancy and anguish, in superearthly exaltation and transfigured grief—the ripening "flame upon the bough" of fate and change; until, at the close, she can give such utterance as one had never known to the ultimate sublimity of her *requiescat* to the doomed and waiting god, while we, sitting awed before her, watch and listen and await, in Wagner's apocalyptic vision, the passing of the old order and the coming of the new.

❧   ❧   ❧

Long before the composition of the *Ring* was finished, the cynical and hard-boiled Hans von Bülow wrote of it to a friend, "I cannot talk to you about the *Nibelungen*—in face of this work, all the resources of expression fail one. I will just say this . . . Nothing like it, nothing approaching it, has ever been produced in any tongue, anywhere, at any time. From it one looks right down, right over, everything else."

Such music might conceivably outlast the

race that made it. More than half a century ago, Wagner completed it—a strange, perturbing portent, as it seemed to its contemporaries. Today it has the unmistakable quality of timelessness. Almost one can hear this music murmuring Brünnhilde's words in *Siegfried,* "Ewig war ich, ewig bin ich."

The most inspired of American writers once said of the potency of music in general something that applies with special relevance to Wagner's music in the *Ring:* Of all that one had imagined concerning heroism, he said, it reminds and reassures one; it makes, for a time, one's dreams and visions seem the only real experience; it prompts one's faith to so wide an elasticity that only the unbelievable will satisfy; it tells one again to trust the remotest, as the divinest, instinct; it is a life unlived save by the greatness of the imagination, a life beyond life, "where at length one's years might pass."

VIII

"Tristan und Isolde"

IT IS one of the supremely ironic jests of musical history that Wagner at one time thought of his projected *Tristan und Isolde* as a sort of lyrico-dramatic potboiler.

In the well-known letter which he wrote to Liszt from Zürich on June 28, 1857, telling him that he had "decided to abandon" his "obstinate attempt" to complete the *Ring,* and that he had stopped work on the composition of *Siegfried,* he added: "I hope I may be justified in supposing that a thoroughly practicable work, such as *Tristan* is to be, will speedily yield good revenues, and keep me afloat for a while."

"My idea this time," he wrote a few months later to a member of the publishing firm of Breitkopf and Härtel, "is to make things attractive and easy. The warm interest of my subject, its happy adaptation to a melodious flow in musical treatment, the effective leading roles, which should rapidly take their places among the most inviting parts open to our sopranos and tenors—all this satisfies me that, without having especially sought it, I have gone the right way to secure a remarkable popular success . . ." [1]

"While *Tristan* is letting the world hear something from me again," he wrote Frau Julie Ritter in October, 1857, "I shall go on forging the great work [the *Ring*], for which, however, I must first suitably prepare the world before I can present it."

Wagner's new opus, as Thomas Mann remarks, "was to be something almost Italian in character, something tuneful, lyrical, and singable, with a small cast, easy to produce, quite simple; . . . a mere operatic romance, with Tristan and Isolde as the conventional lovers of the lyric stage, gratifying a guilty passion and singing melodiously about it for our benefit: and the result is—*Tristan*. One cannot make oneself

---

[1] Wagner in his Autobiography says that he conceived his *Tristan* in 1854, while he was composing the music of *Die Walküre*. The *Tristan* prose-sketch and the dramatic poem itself were written in August and September, 1857. The pencilled composition-sketches, which Mathilde Wesendonck went over with pen and ink to insure their permanence, were dated by Wagner himself as follows: Act I, October 1 to December 31, 1857; Act II, May 4 to July 1, 1858; Act III, April 9 to July 16, 1859. The orchestral-sketches were written between November 5, 1857, and July 19, 1859. The full score was completed at the Hotel Schweizerhof, Lucerne, August 6, 1859. This date, with the initials "R.W.," is inscribed at the bottom of the last page in the Autograph copy of the score—although Wagner, who was occasionally inaccurate in such matters, wrote in a letter to the Princess Marie Wittgenstein dated August 8th: "Yesterday I finished the score of *Tristan.*" The opera was not heard until almost six years later, when it was produced at Munich, June 10, 1865, under Bülow.

smaller than one is: one does what one is; and art is truth—the truth about the artist."

For it goes without saying that Wagner, being what he was, responded to other than merely practical considerations when he broke off his work on the *Ring* in 1857 to compose *Tristan.* He made clear in later years the variety of reasons that had impelled him. Writing [2] in the year after the completion of *Tristan,* he tells us that "the outward motive" for the interruption of the *Ring* by *Tristan* was "the desire to provide a work whose stage requirements and compass should make it sooner and more easily performable"; but the wish was "inspired by the need to hear once more something of my own. Encouraging accounts of performances of my older works in Germany seemed to give this wish a possibility of fulfillment." He reminds us, in his *Epilogue to the Nibelung's Ring* (1871), that when, "by the summer of 1857," he "had completed the music of *Das Rheingold, Die Walküre,* and a large portion of *Siegfried,* eight long years had elapsed since any performance of a dramatic work of mine had exercised its quickening influence on my senses, and through them on my powers of conception. Only under the greatest difficulty had it been possible for me, from time to time, to hear even the sound of an orchestra . . ." And, in a famous

[2] In *Zukunftsmusik.*

and touching sentence, he adds: ". . . Thus, when I laid one silent score upon another, . . . even to myself at times I appeared like one who walks in sleep, unconscious of his actions." No wonder he saw in the completion of *Tristan* not only a means of reëstablishing his contact with the outer world, but the satisfaction of an inner and tyrannical impulse of his own creative will.

Thus *Tristan,* the promising potboiler, became what Wagner was obliged by imperious inner necessity to make it: a work belonging among the purest and loftiest testaments of the creative mind, exerting that special function which was ascribed to antique tragedy: a true *katharsis,* achieved in that ultimate stillness of the spirit where pity and fear perform their lustral office and "lead the soul to peace." Moreover, *Tristan* embodies that exalted conception of the art of the stage which guided Wagner, consciously or unconsciously, throughout the greater part of his life: that view of the lyric theatre as akin to the theatre of the Greeks—as the source and generator of uniting imaginative experience. For, as John Dewey has remarked, "in Athens, which we regard as the home par excellence of epic and lyric poetry, of the arts, of drama, architecture, and sculpture, the idea of art for art's sake would not have been understood . . . Drama was enacted on holy-days; attendance was of the nature of an act of civic worship."

Wagner was forty-six when he set down the last note of the orchestral score of *Tristan*. He lived to be nearly seventy—lived to become the composer of the greatest comedy in music, *Die Meistersinger,* and the greatest tragedy, *Götterdämmerung;* lived to become the tranquillized seer of *Parsifal,* with all of life and wisdom spread open to his compassionate understanding: yet *Tristan,* this work of his middle age, soars upward from his creative history like a pillar of flame, a thing so incandescent and unquenchable that men cannot yet look upon it with untroubled eyes.

Tristan is unique not only among Wagner's works, but among all outgivings of the musical mind, because it is devoted, with an exclusiveness and concentration and intensity beyond comparison, to the rendering of essential experience. Wagner is concerned here not with epic paragons, or elemental beings of fire and of the depths, or gods and goddesses, or a cosmos in distress, or some brilliant and crowded chapter out of a romantic past: but with the inner life of life itself. In this score, he is at the summit of his genius. These passionate transvaluations of love and death have called forth the greatest that he could give; and he has steeped this miraculous music in a beauty that is outside of time.

☙ ☙ ☙

Doubtless there will always be dispute among students and historians concerning that unanswered and unanswerable question—the extent to which Wagner's Zürich inamorata, Mathilde Wesendonck, was responsible for the creation of *Tristan und Isolde*. It has long been assumed that Wagner was afire with his passion for Mathilde, and was driven to assuage and sublimate his agony by turning it into music. But perhaps the aesthetic psychologists are nearer the truth when they say that Wagner was afire with the music of *Tristan,* and sought a human torch to bear the flame. "When Nature has made us ripe for love," remarked the acutest of novelistic philosophers, "it is seldom that the Fates are behindhand in furnishing a temple for the flame." Wagner, to be sure, was perpetually ripe for love. But there are degrees; and in 1857 he was riper for it than usual. *Tristan* was, perhaps, both torch and flame.

What Arthur Symons pointed out when Wagner's letters and journals written to and for Mathilde, those confessions of inimitable and affecting sincerity and feeling, first appeared in English, more than a quarter of a century ago, is still, I think, discerning and beyond dispute—that

Mathilde Wesendonck "came into Wagner's life precisely when his genius required her, and dropped out of it precisely when her service was accomplished. People have spent much needless trouble in trying to determine whether Wagner's wife Minna had what is called 'good justification' for being jealous of Mathilde Wesendonck, and Otto Wesendonck for being jealous of Wagner. The main result, at all events, is summed up in two phrases: one, written by Wagner in 1861: 'For my having written *Tristan,* I thank you from my deepest soul to all eternity'; and the other, written by Mathilde in 1862: 'As long as breath is in me, I shall aspire and strive on; and that is your doing.' "

Their propinquity, at least, came to an end on August 17, 1858, when Wagner (with the score of *Tristan's* First Act safely in his publishers' hands and the composition-sketch of the Second Act in his gripsack) left Zürich in the early morning, after his wife had made a cup of tea for him, and walked with him in the garden, and accompanied him to the railroad station, when she broke out into bitter reproaches as he went away alone, bound ultimately for Venice. "Then, and for long afterwards," remarked Mr. Symons, "Wagner believed himself to be passionately in love with his friend's wife; he believed that he was tearing himself away from temptation; that

he was renouncing his life's happiness. And it was
well that he believed it, for the mental agony all
went straight into *Tristan* and helped to fit it for
immortality. But though Wagner renounced the
woman, he could not have renounced *Tristan*.
Tangled on all sides, he breaks every bond, and is
free, free to write his music. He tears himself
from Zürich with distress, but he never asks the
woman to follow him, and it is quite evident that
he never wishes it. It is doubtful if she would
have followed him. As he wrote afterwards, she
was full of 'beautiful aesthetic calm'; she was an
exquisite friend; she loved him, no doubt . . .
But she was no Isolde. They profited in their own
ways: she gained an ideal, and he an achievement."

Mr. Symons could naturally not have known
what Wagner said privately about the matter
fourteen years later to his beloved Cosima, after
he had married her and they were living in Bayreuth, and he was completing *Götterdämmerung,*
and she was keeping that invaluable diary of their
life together which Count Du Moulin-Eckart
gave us in tantalizing fragments a few years ago.
"It is only when one grows older," said Wagner
to Cosima, "that one understands one's own life.
When I think of the force which urged me to
sketch out the plan of *Tristan,* just when you and
Hans [von Bülow] paid your first visit to Zürich,

whereas up to that time I had been quietly completing two Acts of *Siegfried;* and when I survey the whole sequence of events up to the performance of *Tristan* at Munich, I can see how everything is psychical, and how deceptive is all that falls under the category of the conscious. How different it would appear to one who could survey the whole as though it were revealed in a moment! There was the germ of an immense passion within me, as in Romeo, but my conscious mind took it for a feeling of tenderness toward Rosaline."

It is interesting to compare this explanation —so tactful in its emphasis upon the potentiality of his love for Cosima, and its veiled but minimizing allusion to Mathilde—with the explanation contained in Wagner's letter written to Mathilde herself from Venice, January 19, 1859, while he was at work on the orchestral-sketches of the Second Act of *Tristan.* He is speaking of the peculiar nature of the poet, of the artistic creator, "forever unintelligible to the ordinary man." The usual view of life, he says, "turns on the pivot of experience; whereas the intuition of the artist-mind, preceding all experience, embraces that which lends experience a meaning. It is independent of space and time and causality. As Schiller so finely says, it alone is true because it never *was:* this Something that is surer and more definite than any other object of cognition, though it has

153

not a single attribute of the world which we know by experience. This is surprisingly true in my own case. My poetic conceptions have always been . . . far in advance of my experience. *The Flying Dutchman, Tannhäuser, Lohengrin,* the *Nibelungen,* . . . were all of them in my mind before they became part of my experience. Perhaps you can feel for yourself in what a wonderful relationship I now stand to *Tristan.* I say it openly— since it is an observation due to the initiated, if not to the world—that never has an idea become so definitely an experience. How far the two, the idea and the experience, were mutually predestined, is a subject of such subtlety that the ordinary processes of thought could present it only in a distorted form. And now, when Savitri [3] and Parzival [4] are striving to take imaginative shape —when I bend brooding in formative stillness over the completion of my *Tristan*—who can imagine the wonder that fills me, and withdraws me so completely from the world that I have already overcome it? *You* can divine it, *you* know it! Yes, and probably you alone! . . ."

This, to be sure, is not the plainest sort of statement. But Wagner was dealing with fugitive

[3] Prakriti (otherwise Savitri) was the heroine of Wagner's projected Buddhistic drama, *Die Sieger* (*The Victors*), the scenario of which he sketched in May, 1856, the year before he began his work on *Tristan.*

[4] Wagner's early spelling of the name.

and difficult ideas; and, as is often the case when
we read his deliverances, we should remember the
crisply conclusive observation of Mrs. Moun-
stuart-Jenkinson: "My remarks are thrown out to
be apprehended, and not dissected." What Wagner
meant to suggest, probably, was that the creation
of *Tristan* and his own relationship with Mathilde
were not cause and consequence, but a kind of
mystical and predestined convergence of intuition
and experience.

❦   ❦   ❦

Which brings us face to face with the truth
that it is impossible to understand the basic conceptions of Wagner's dramas and music, from
The Flying Dutchman to *Parsifal,* without knowing something about the ideas that formed so increasingly influential a part of his thinking during the years of his maturity.

The true action of *Tristan,* of the *Ring,* of
Parsifal, even of *Die Meistersinger,* is interior.
Wagner was fundamentally a mystic; and we cannot hope to comprehend his dramas and the inter-
action between them and his music unless we are
willing and able to grant him his philosophical
premises, and place ourselves, with him, at the
centre of his conceptions and their working-out.

An adequately correlating study of the fundamental and inseparable relationship between the

155

later music-dramas—in particular, the *Ring, Tristan, Parsifal*—and those ancient religions and literatures of the East which progressively influenced Wagner's mind, has yet to be made in English. The profounder Oriental teachings are outside the usual range of musical scholarship—to say nothing of the fact that their comprehension would involve the study of a lifetime; and Western specialists in Eastern mysticism have, as a rule, but the dimmest awareness of the intellectual and spiritual content of Occidental music.

In Wagner's case, the whole subject has been unhappily confused by the persistence with which too-casual observers have repeated the dreary chatter about Schopenhauer's presumably controlling part in shaping the ideology of *Tristan* and the *Ring*. It is commonly supposed and often asserted that Wagner derived the philosophical ideas which underlie the drama and music of *Tristan,* in particular, from the author of *Die Welt als Wille und Vorstellung,* and that those ideas, as Wagner expressed them in *Tristan,* are profoundly pessimistic. Both these suppositions are highly debatable. In the first place, the idea of spiritual consummation and appeasement through a mystical Death-in-Love was in Wagner's mind —and is to be found in his writings—before he had even heard of Schopenhauer. In 1851, shortly after he had completed *Lohengrin,* and when he

was shaping the dramas that were eventually to
be the *Ring,* we find him using these words: "This
love-yearning, the noblest thing my heart could
feel,—what other could it be than a longing for
release from the present, for absorption in an element of infinite love, a love not to be found on
earth, and reaching through the gates of Death
alone?"

This, as other Wagerian students have
pointed out, is an expression of the idea that was
afterward to form the basis of *Tristan*—one can
almost hear, turned into prose, the very words of
the lovers in the garden. Yet Wagner, at the time,
knew nothing whatever of Schopenhauer. Later,
in 1854, after his first reading of *The World as
Will and Idea,* he wrote to Liszt: "His [Schopen-
hauer's] chief idea, the final negation of the desire of life, is terribly serious, but it indicates the
only salvation possible. To me, of course, that
thought was not new."

Wagner, admittedly, was fascinated by
Schopenhauer's *Welt als Wille und Vorstellung*
when he encountered it in 1854 (while he was
working on the composition-sketch of *Die Walküre*); and a few years later he was generous
enough to say that from Schopenhauer he had
learnt to understand his own works, and had been
enabled to comprehend them with his reason as
well as with his intuition. Yet it was not primarily

from the pessimistic and defeatist philosophy of Schopenhauer that Wagner derived the inner substance of *Tristan* and, in part, of the *Ring* and *Parsifal,* but from the mystical doctrines of the East, those profound and noble concepts of enlightened wisdom and the spiritual destiny of man which suffered so curious and depressing a sea-change when they passed through Schopenhauer's mind. Wagner must have been dazzled indeed by the brilliance of Schopenhauer's writing; for it was scarcely necessary for him to give credit to Schopenhauer for ideas which had already come to him from the source which had been drawn upon by them both [5]—those philosophical speculations of ancient India, into which the poet-composer had penetrated so much more deeply and intuitively than had the philosopher whom he admired and praised. For not only the exaltation of Wagner's greater works themselves, but his letters and prose works and the records of his sayings, give us proof of his absorption in the literature of the East, and his understanding of its luminous and lofty valor.

[5] Schopenhauer's attention had been directed to the philosophy of the ancient Hindus in his twenty-fifth year, at Weimar, by the Orientalist F. Mayer, through Friedrich Schlegel's *Language and Wisdom of the Old Hindus* and Anquetil Duperron's version of the Upanishads. This was about a quarter of a century before the embittered philosopher settled at Frankfort, and, as Professor Wallace observes in his biography, "found his trustiest mate in a poodle."

We find him urging Mathilde, in the Zürich period, to command Otto to procure for her "at once" the "Hindu legends edited by Adolf Holtz-mann," and assuring her that "our whole culture stands shamed by these purest revelations of no-blest humanity in the ancient East." A year later (1856) he is sketching the scenario of his pro-jected Buddhist drama, *Die Sieger,* which he never carried further, but some of whose ele-ments, as I have already pointed out, found their way into *Tristan* and *Parsifal;* and soon after, he drafts that mystical variant (afterward aban-doned) of Brünnhilde's farewell oration in *Göt-terdämmerung* to which I referred in the preced-ing chapter—words that are meaningless to those who are unfamiliar with the Hindu doctrines of Karma and rebirth. Writing to Mathilde from Lucerne in 1859, he compliments her upon finding her way through Köppen's *History of the Reli-gion of Buddha,* and bursts into a paean in praise of that view of the world [Buddhism] "compared with which all other dogmas must surely look parochial and petty. The philosopher with his broader thought," he continues, "the explorer of Nature with his most extensive deductions, the artist with his most transcendent imaginings, the man with the wisest heart for all that breathes and suffers—all find in this wondrous and quite

incomparable world-myth a home the least con-
fined, and in it their whole selves again."

The opening of the *Tristan* Prelude is explained to Mathilde, seven months after the completion of the opera, in Hindu terminology: "I
often look towards the land of Nirvana," writes
Wagner. "Nirvana in its turn, however, soon
changes into *Tristan*—you know the Buddhist
theory of the world's creation: A breath perturbs
the heaven's translucence [here Wagner quotes
in musical notation the first ascending chromatic
phrase of the oboe, bars three and four—sometimes called the motive of Isolde's Magic]. It
swells, condenses, and at last the whole world
stands forth in prisoning solidity."

From Paris, where he is engrossed in the
preparation of *Tannhäuser* for production at the
Opéra, he writes Mathilde (at the beginning of
August, 1860) concerning "the profound hypothesis of Reincarnation," which alone has been
able, he says, to show him "the consoling point
where all souls converge in the end to an equal
height of redemption, after their diverse lives,
running separately though side by side in Time,
have met in full awareness beyond it. On that
beautiful Buddhist hypothesis, the spotless purity
of Lohengrin becomes easy to explain, in that he
is the continuation of Parzival [*sic*]—who had

first to achieve his purity. In the same sense
would Elsa reach up to Lohengrin in her rebirth.
Thus the plan for my *Sieger* would appear to me
the sequel and conclusion of *Lohengrin:* here
Savitri (corresponding to Elsa) fully overtakes
Ananda. Thus the awful tragedy of life arises
from separateness in time and space; but since
time and space are nothing but our mode of ap-
prehension, and have no reality apart from that,
so to the men of clearest perception even the utmost tragic grief should be explainable as only
the individual's defect of vision. So it is, I believe."

Fourteen years later, at Bayreuth in 1874,
when Wagner, with all his works save *Parsifal*
composed, was within a decade of his end, we find
him "absorbed," with Cosima, in that long-famil-
iar world of Hindu literature, and discovering in
it "the great thoughts that guided him as man
and artist." On the night before his death at Venice, Cosima heard him speaking, and went into
his room. He told her that he had been talking
about her, and embraced her long and tenderly.
"Every five thousand years it is a success," he
said, thinking of their marriage. Cosima records
in her diary that she "spoke of the Hindu nature,
and of how the soul longs for its other soul."

❧   ❧   ❧

In one of his essays (*Zukunftsmusik*), Wagner is speaking of the destructive power of doubt, and its effect on Elsa, and he tells us that it beset him also as a creative artist. But all doubt forsook him, he says, when at last he gave himself up to *Tristan:* "Here, in absolute faith, I plunged into the profoundest depths of the spirit, and fashioned the outward semblance of the work from the inmost centre of that realm . . . Life and Death, the whole meaning and existence of the outer world, here depend entirely on the hidden mysteries of the spirit. It is the desire of the inmost soul itself that brings about the affecting action of the drama, and it enters the light of day precisely as it was shaped beforehand in that inner shrine."

That "shaping," in the last analysis, is musical. By a kind of miraculous process of aesthetic transubstantiation, unapproached before or since, Wagner, as I have tried to make clear in an earlier chapter, converts his drama into music. One remembers that passage from Emerson's *Society and Solitude:* "Her speech flows like a river. . . . It is a true substantiation—the fact converted into speech, all warm and colored." With Wagner, the drama and its elements—its action and speech and setting, its implications and its silences —have their concurrent and transformed counterpart in the music, which becomes an order of dramatic symphony with obbligato voice-parts.

Thus it follows, as we have reminded ourselves elsewhere in these chapters, that the sheer musician in Wagner is dominant and prevailing. It is easy to feel that his unexampled scores— those subtle and immense designs, with their inexhaustible, unfolding patterns of expressive tone —are their own excuse for being. In *Tristan,* the unabridged duet, with its wondrous fantasia upon the interwoven themes of Night and Day, Love and Death, is alone enough to persuade us that this music remains the most magical efflorescence that the art of music has attained: the triumphant achievement, as a great poet said concerning Shelley's poetry, "of the utmost beauty possible to human utterance." The colloquy of the desperate, enraptured lovers in the garden, "remembering how brief the whole of joy, which its own hours annihilate"; the voice of the watcher on the tower borne to us across an orchestral nocturne in which all the nameless mystery and enchantment of the night are concentrated into less than half a hundred bars, whose woven melodies twine about Brangäne's dreamlike song as if they were the interlacing voices of the fountain and the coming dawn and the encircling trees: music whose beauty, like Juliet's, hangs upon the cheek of night—such pages yield to the music lover a depth and intensity of experience that becomes, for many, almost unendurable.

Certainly it is possible to sit before such music, entranced and overborne, with small concern for what it signifies, indifferent to everything except the superhuman beauty of the tonal web—indifferent to the meaning of the lovers' dialogue, neither knowing nor caring why Tristan seeks death at Melot's hands, nor why the music at one point or another takes the course it does. But this is not to get from Wagner all that he can give us. His music, as such, is incomparable and possessing, but it is also a vehicle of communication: and what it says, in addition to what it is, becomes indispensable for those who wish to hear.

The Wagner of *Tristan und Isolde* "caught up the whole of love and uttered it": this music is the last word that any art has thus far spoken about the anguish and the ecstasy of human passion. But to look upon *Tristan* as nothing more than a glorification of passionate and tragic human love is scarcely to see below its surface. It is that, of course; and one might reasonably feel that that, in all conscience, should be enough to satisfy anyone. But Wagner happens to have made *Tristan* something more than a lyric tragedy of passionate and fateful love. He conceived it as a drama of the inner life of man; and unless

164

we realize that truth, and are moved by that reality, we get only the exterior of the work—overwhelming as that is.

The so-called "love duet," for instance, is no such thing, in the usual operatic sense. That unprecedented dialogue is an interchange of feeling and experience between two nobly tragic natures who find themselves confronting the profoundest realities and mysteries of the spirit. Wagner has made this clear in the passage quoted on an earlier page, in which he tells us that in *Tristan* the whole meaning and existence of the outer world depend entirely on the hidden mysteries of the spirit's life.

One may speak of *Tristan,* if one wishes, as "erotic"; but that is to note what is perhaps its least important characteristic—unless one applies the term in its strictly derivative sense, remembering all that Eros meant for the ancients: that he stood for the most exalted conception of love, "so divine and impersonal as but faintly to be comprehended by finite minds." It was Wagner himself who referred to another phase of his symbolic treatment of the music-drama's theme when he remarked to a friend for whom he was playing *Tristan* that "the ancients represented Eros as the genius of death, with a reversed torch in his hand": and it is the motive of Death—sung by Isolde in the second scene of the First Act to the

words, "Tod-geweihtes Haupt" ("Death-devoted
Head")—that we hear on the trumpets, in combination with the motive of the Torch on the
descending woodwinds, as Isolde in Act II extinguishes the flame whose darkening will signal the
waiting Tristan to her side.

❧   ❧   ❧

Wagner conceived his *Tristan* as a mystery-
play, a parable of the deepest longing and aspiration of the human mind: for the central argu-
ment of *Tristan* stems from the timeless Wisdom
of the East. It is as old as the Upanishads, and
as modern as Shelley. Wagner has prefigured in
symbols of overmastering power the immortal
protest of the human spirit against its doom of
separateness, and the answer that resolves it.
From the opening measures of the Prelude we are
made aware of the terrible disquiet that is to agi-
tate the music recurrently as the lovers come to
understand that all delight and all enchantment
are no more than "a dream that lingers a moment
. . . a breath, a flame in the doorway," until the
éclaircissement at the end—the death-song of
Isolde, with its mood of luminous revelation and
appeasement in which Wagner has prisoned forever the wonderment of seers and poets at "the
idleness of tears." Who that has witnessed in the
opera house the music-drama's close can ever dis-

166

lodge the memory of Isolde, oblivious of all around her, as she sinks at the end upon Tristan's body, while the music, out of its secret wisdom, utters its corroborative word: "I and this Love are one, and I am Death"; or can forget the sound of the transported orchestra as it comes to a close upon that irradiated final chord whose sound is like no other in the whole of music, while we watch the daylight fade, and know that all desire and all regret have become as a quiet fold of evening sky?

The mystery of love, said a second-rate writer in a moment of first-rate inspiration, is greater than the mystery of death. It is a saying that Wagner's lovers, and their wise, ancestral prototypes, and Wagner himself, would not have questioned. They are distraught, these complementary spirits, by their inappeasable desire for an unflawed realization of their love. But the impassable barrier becomes apparent: they are two separate beings, and not one indivisible entity. Their duality stands between them, and they long to escape the insufferable solitude of individual existence. They would achieve what the author of *Religio Medici* had in mind when he wrote, almost three centuries ago, that "there are wonders in true affection: it is a body of enigmas, mysteries, and riddles, wherein two so become one. . . ."

Concerning the profound and esoteric con-

167

cept involved in Wagner's solution of the psychic impasse reached by the lovers in his spiritual fable, wherein he touches hands with the sages and mystics of the ageless East, Wagner himself, happily for us, has spoken confirmingly in certain comments upon *Tristan*.

Eager to hear at least the Prelude to his score, he planned to perform it at the first of three concerts which he arranged to give at Paris in the Winter of 1859-60, five months after the completion of the opera. "You know," he wrote Mathilde Wesendonck in December, "that Hans [von Bülow] wanted to conduct the Prelude last winter, and begged me to write a [concert] ending for it.[6] At that time I had no idea for such an ending, and it seemed so impossible that I flatly declined. Since then, however, I have written the Third Act, and have found the full close for the whole [the finale of the opera, Isolde's deathsong]. So, while drawing up the program for a Paris concert—the particular incentive to which was my desire to get a hearing of the *Tristan* Prelude—it occurred to me to intimate that close in advance, as a glimmering presage of deliverance. Well, it has succeeded quite admirably, and

[6] The *Tristan* Prelude was conducted by Bülow, for the first time anywhere, at a concert in Prague, March 12, 1859, more than five months before Wagner finished the opera—he had not even begun the composition-sketches of Act III. Bülow wrote his own close for the Prelude, but Wagner's is the only one published.

today I send you this mysteriously tranquillizing close as the best gift I can make for your birthday. I have written the piece out for you pretty much as I play it to myself on the pianoforte. . . . Now see what you can make of the onerous present!"

Wagner enclosed with his letter to Mathilde not only the piano transcription of the concert-ending which he had devised for the Prelude, but an "explanation" of the music of the Prelude as a whole. He wrote this explanation, in his enviably clear and beautiful calligraphy, on the back of the sheet of manuscript music containing the concert-close of the Prelude.[7] It is even more indispensable for our enlightenment concerning *Tristan* than it can have been for Mathilde's: for it gives us a clue to that inner action of the drama which, as Wagner elsewhere tells us, shaped its outer form.

Here is the essential part of his explanation (the opening paragraph, which I omit, is an outline of the drama down to the moment of the drinking of the philtre):

". . . The passion of the lovers mounts suddenly to vivid flame, and each avows to each that they belong to none save one another. Henceforth

[7] Both the music and the explanation are given in facsimile in the English edition of Wagner's Letters to Mathilde Wesendonck, translated by William Ashton Ellis. (London, H. Grevel & Co., 1905.)

there is no end to the yearning, the bliss, the
misery of love. The world, power, fame, splendor,
honor, knighthood, loyalty, friendship—all are
scattered like a baseless dream. One thing only
remains: desire, desire unquenchable, forever
born anew . . . one sole redemption—Death,
surcease of being, deliverance.

"Here, in the boundless realm of Music's
very element, the musician who chose this theme
for the Prelude to his drama could have but one
care: how he should set bounds to his fancy; since
the exhaustion of the theme was impossible.
Thus he took, once for all, this insatiable desire.
In long-drawn accents he let that unslaked longing swell from its first timid avowal, through
gentle sighs, hopes, and fears, laments and wishes,
joy and torment, up to the mightiest onslaught,
the most powerful endeavor to find the breach
that would open to the heart the ocean of the
endless joy of love. In vain! Its power spent, the
heart sinks back, to pine with desire, with desire
unfulfilled; since each fruition only brings forth
seeds of fresh desire. Till, at last, in the depth of
its exhaustion, the starting eye sees the glimmering of the highest bliss of attainment. It is the
ecstasy of dying, of the surrender of being, of
the final redemption into that wondrous realm
from which we wander farthest when we strive
to take it by force. Shall we call this death? Is it

not rather the wonder-world of night, out of which, so says the story, the ivy and the vine sprang forth in tight embrace over the tomb of Tristan and Isolde?" [8]

That "glimmering of the highest bliss of attainment," of "the ecstasy of dying," which Wagner refers to here, finds no expression in the *Tristan* Prelude as we hear it in its original and familiar form, either in the opera house as introduction to the First Act of the music-drama, or in its usual association with the music of Isolde's so-called "Liebestod," [9] with which it is almost invariably linked in the concert-room. The "glimmering of the highest bliss of attainment" is to be discovered only in the seldom-heard concert version of the Prelude which Wagner devised for his Paris concert, with the specially written ending.

Wagner's phrase, "the highest bliss of attainment," has a curiously exact parallel in one of the Eastern scriptures; and it is hard to believe that Wagner, to whom the sacred literature

[8] "In ancient Greek symbology, Dionysus (or Bacchus, the Vine) crowned with Ivy, represented the 'Anointed' or perfect being. The later signification of Bacchus was a degenerate one, and had nothing whatever to do with the pure and original Dionysus, whose altar stood within the circle of the tragic chorus" (A. L. Cleather).

[9] The name Liebestod, now universally applied to Isolde's death-song, was not given to it by Wagner, who associated that name with the Prelude to the music-drama, while he called the finale *Verklärung* (Transfiguration).

of the Hindus was an open book, did not have that passage definitely in mind when he was writing his explanation for Mathilde. It cannot be too often emphasized that the true parallel to the philosophy of *Tristan* is to be found in the ancient mystical writings of the East, rather than in Schopenhauer's brilliant but superficial variations upon a system of ideas with which Wagner was already familiar when Schopenhauer first dawned upon his mental world. Wagner would certainly have written, in some form, a *Tristan* and a *Ring* if he had never read a word of Schopenhauer or heard of his philosophy.

Whether that mystical conception of spiritual consummation upon which he based the dramatic and musical structure of *Tristan* is or is not "pessimistic" remains a point upon which students of Eastern thought are not agreed. Some of the most enlightened and profound among them have found those Indian teachings full of high and kindling wisdom, full of exalted courage and the noblest aspiration. Nirvana does not, they tell us, mean annihilation: it means fulfillment and realization —the full and present eternity of life. "Not wisdom, or love, or beauty, or power, but all in one, is that for which all things exist." Hearing Isolde's death-song, the student of Eastern thought recalls the question asked of the Vedic Master by Sâuryâyanin Gârgya, and the sage's answer:

"Who is the shining one who sees dreams? Whose is that bliss? And in whom are these set firm?"

"As, Gârgya, the rays of the sun, at setting, all become one in the shining orb, and when he rises, all come forth again, so all becomes one in the being that is made radiant. . . . The seen and the unseen, heard and unheard, enjoyed and unenjoyed, real and unreal, he sees it all; as All he sees it. And when he is wrapped by the radiance, the shining one no longer sees dreams. Then within him the bliss arises"—wherewith we come again almost to Wagner's very words.

Wagner espoused many doctrines in the course of his tireless intellectual life; but none survived so long or made so deep an impress on his work as those teachings which he absorbed from his studies in the sacred literature of the East—"the oldest and holiest of human religions," as he called it; and Wagner the mystical philosopher conditioned the dramas and the music of the greater works. Always he had the mystic's assured perception of reality. Always, as in *Tristan,* he spoke from "the mind of the mind."

❦   ❦   ❦

Those who have lived with *Tristan* closest and longest are increasingly puzzled by that once-accepted view of it as largely the overripe fruit of a voluptuous imagination—music that is streaked with sensuality. George Moore, in the unregenerate days of romantic Wagnerian criticism, voiced this conception when, in an empurpled fantasy, he personified the music of Wagner as "a Turk lying amid the houris promised by the prophet to the Faithful," surrounded by "the motley morbidity of figs, the passion of red pomegranates"—music with "cruel claws and amorous tongue that feeds upon my flesh."

Whatever inclination Wagner the human being may sometimes have had toward the passionate pomegranates and the morbid figs of life (a matter which it is not within the province of these studies to discuss), it is certain that the real Wagner, Wagner the artist, did not sit for the portrait so delightedly painted by Mr. Moore.

Wagner's style at its most typical is essentially a noble and exalted one. To identify the rapturous beauty of the music of *Tristan* with the sort of voluptuous hashish dream that Mr. Moore thought relevant to its character was a feat that would probably be impossible today for enlightened connoisseurs of Wagner, to whom the graver qualities of this music—its sorrowful grandeur, its power and weight of speech, its tragic elevation—are increasingly apparent. An illustrious interpreter of Wagner once gave to

174

this deponent his view of *Tristan:* "Ever since I first conducted Wagner's masterpiece many years ago," he wrote, "it has seemed to me that this music is pervaded from the start by a presentiment of tragic fatefulness; and I have always sought, in conducting it, to emphasize that quality in the music which relates it to the greatness of antique tragedy."

I think that is a sound and sensitive judgment. Wagner's magnificence, of course, is undebatable. The loftiness of his sublimer pages, their noble and prophetic grandeur, are luminous with the glow reflected from a musical texture of the utmost complexity and richness. Yet when one has finished marvelling (if one ever does) at their splendor and loveliness of imagery, the long, prismatic cadences in which chord melts into chord "as color melts into color in the sunset," there remain the sweep and vastness of the architectural design, the granite and the tempered steel behind the tapestries and jewels and the woven gold. For Wagner can be, when he wishes, as elemental and severe and toweringly bare as Homer or Beethoven or Bach.

His art, like those of other geniuses, is protean. Certain works are multiple, exhaustless, ever-changing: they are not, as we sometimes think, static and changeless. As one or another re-creative mind is brought to bear on them, as one period or another of aesthetic history submits them to its own peculiar scale of values, new aspects of them come to view, their contents change, their meanings alter. They may deepen and expand in various surprising ways as one light or another falls upon their surfaces and penetrates their depths. As Lytton Strachey wrote about poetic tragedy: "It is not only immortal; it is also forever new. There are infinite implications in it which reveal themselves by a mysterious law to each succeeding generation. The *Oedipus* acted yesterday at Cambridge was the identical play that won the prize two thousand years ago; and yet it was a different *Oedipus,* with meanings for the modern audience which were unperceived by the Athenians. The records show conclusively that the Phèdre of Bernhardt differed as much from that of Rachel as that of Rachel differed from Clarion's, and as Clarion's differed from that of the great actress who created the part under the eyes of Racine. But each was Phèdre."

It is possible that Mr. Strachey, like most men of letters, did not look upon music as one of the major arts; and so I do not know if he would have been graciously willing to regard it as among the proper vehicles of tragedy, along with literature and the drama. Yet it is true, I think, that music is inexhaustible and protean in a sense that is not true of any other art. There may be a

dozen different significations in the tragedy of
Oedipus. But I doubt whether a tragic drama,
with its relatively fixed and definite patterns of
expression, could ever be made to yield the variety
of suggestion and significance that is implicit in,
for example, the music of *Tristan und Isolde*.

Music, let us remember, is that art which
speaks by proxy, or through deputies.

"Absent thee from felicity awhile." . . . The
words need only be printed marks upon the page,
yet we are instantly smitten through and through
by all that they hold of sharp intolerable beauty:
we need not wait until some actor speaks them
from a stage. But what is the Prelude to *Tristan
und Isolde* as Wagner left it to the world? A
brief, mysterious, incandescent pattern of inestimable beauty (you may reply), growing out
of the darkness of silence and returning into it.
Not at all. What Wagner left us, and all that he
left us, is a complex of hieroglyphics on white
paper, telling the reader of his signs that Wagner
wanted B to sound with F, or A-sharp to follow
A. It is not until some talented first oboist, directed by some conductor of musical sensibility
and insight, actually causes A-sharp to follow A,
that *Tristan* begins to stir and wake and live.
For Wagner, after all, wrote his music to be
heard. It is true that some of us, happily independent of oboists and conductors, can re-create

his music for ourselves from the orchestral score
before us on our study table. We may thus have
heard *Tristan* in a hundred of those silent performances which musicians like to attend in the
quiet of their own seclusion; and on some favor-
ing night of Summer or of Winter stillness, when
there was no music near at hand except the unheard singing of the instruments or voices from
the lifeless page, we may have felt that for moments we sat, listening, within hearing distance of
that secret place, walled and inaccessible, where
the Wagner of *Tristan* communed apart. Yet even
then we were hearing *Tristan* through the media
of our own peculiar and interposing selves.

"Sehr mässig" ("Very moderate") is the
tempo mark at the beginning of the Liebestod.
But "very moderate," even in a world more definite and palpable than that of music, may mean
one thing to Signor Mussolini, and quite another
thing to Bertrand Russell. Is it any wonder that
the Liebestod, as we hear it conveyed through the
temperaments and prepossessions of various conductors of unquestionable sensibility, so seldom
conforms to one central and governing conception? Is it any wonder that many of us, after
countless hearings, find ourselves asking, "What
is the true *Tristan?* What, in this case, is the
norm?" There may be nine and sixty ways of
constructing tribal lays, and every one of them

may be right; but can there by nine and sixty ways of conceiving the music of *Tristan,* and can each of them be right? If a *Tristan* that comes to our ears as attar of musical poetry, lyricism tipped with flame—if this is the ultimate view of it, what, then, is one to say of that conception which sees it as music of elemental power, huge, titanic, crushing? For I once heard *Tristan* conducted by a master interpreter, in an earlier generation than our own, under whose hands it grew affrightingly into a terrific thing. "This *Tristan* is becoming terrible!" wrote Wagner to Mathilde from Lucerne, in the Spring of 1859, as he worked on the devastating final Act. And the music became terrible under the conductor to whom I listened years ago. For the first time I realized not only the gigantic sweep and the sculpturesque immensity of Wagner's musical design, but I realized that the surpassing loveliness of this score, the enchantment that ravishes the spirit in the Second Act, are perhaps a lesser possession of the work than the greatness of its tragic pathos and its tragic force. I thought, not only in the shattering Third Act, but in the First, of the sculptured agony of Rodin's Dante Gate, with its tortured images of Spirit and Flesh, its sorrowful, transfixing passion.

And as I realized what this singular interpreter was doing—heightening the music to colossal stature, charging it with all the anguish and the passion that men have known in the agonies of love and sorrow—I remembered what a wise man of yesterday had said: "The strong cannot be brave: only the weak can be brave." So, only the cool can burn consumingly. Only the intellectual artist, the ironist, the cool and skeptical thinker, could have unleashed the tempests and the terrors of music such as this without calamity. And such was the interpreter to whom I listened then. His name was Karl Muck, and he was a master. The mere emotionalist, the conductor of mere "temperament," would have drowned in such a flood. The man's impeccable taste, his challenging, astringent malice, shepherded at every point his huge intensities. Yet never before had I heard a reading of such poignant feeling and complete sincerity.

Well, then, is one to say that *Tristan* is Gothic and tremendous, or sensuous and flame-lit and enchanting? I think that one is to say merely that *Tristan* is both of these, and more besides. If one be tempted to object that no single thing could show such differing characters, I suggest that one observe Mont Blanc from Chamonix, and then go down the valley to Combleux and study it from there. It is still Mont Blanc, but one would hardly know it. *Tristan,* like all great music, is illimitable. No one will ever quite see to the end of it, or reach to the bottom or the height of it, or search it in vain for what he thinks is there—granting that he be passionate and humble, sensitive, perceptive, and sincere.

❧　　❧　　❧

Yet this is not to say that Wagner has been unable to leave us in *Tristan,* and in all his scores, certain indications of the most definite and indisputable sort concerning his wishes and intentions; and these we may not ignore without harming the proportions and effect of the music. It is, for example, one of the high virtues of the Metropolitan's latter-day performances of *Tristan* that they have given opportunity to that admirable conductor, Artur Bodanzky, to show us, in a particularly striking and important instance, what it may mean to take Wagner at his word, when that word is explicit and unmistakable and often disregarded. Mr. Bodanzky's musicianly rectitude and his sense of scruple are displayed in this case through the simple process of giving Wagner what he asks.

Some of us who know the score of *Tristan* used to wonder how the Prelude would sound if it were performed throughout in faithful accordance with Wagner's directions as they are recorded on the printed page. The essence of that Prelude is exceptionally difficult to disengage.

The phrases of sorrow and loneliness and aspiration that rise from the orchestra with so indescribable an effect: their mystical suggestion of tonal condensation, of an inner world of being gradually assuming form and substance, symbolizing, as Wagner said, that "perturbing creative breath" which shapes the world and all men's anguish and desire—these musical images are excessively difficult to project. Their effect is immeasurably lessened if Wagner's directions as to the pace of the Prelude are ignored—yet ignored they generally are. It is the almost invariable habit of conductors, even great ones, to disregard Wagner's clear instructions as soon as they get beyond the first half-hundred measures of the Prelude, paying no heed to Wagner's wish that the music be played (after the *a tempo* direction at the forty-sixth bar) without any quickening of the pace. Instead, they begin an accelerando at about the fifty-fourth measure, so that the approach to the great climax sounds almost external and theatrical.

Mr. Bodanzky proceeds otherwise. He seems to have given Wagner credit for knowing what he wanted and how to ask for it. The fact is worthy of note by all lovers and students of Wagner that Mr. Bodanzky at the Metropolitan, almost alone among conductors now active, lets us hear the Prelude played in this respect as Wagner wished. Thus played and heard, the music subdues one by its cumulative weight of tragic passion and inexorable enhancement. It becomes, as it sweeps slowly, overwhelmingly to its apex, a great tide of life ascending from unimaginable depths, a mighty onslaught of the passionate will against the spirit's bounds.

That is what Wagner unquestionably meant and wanted: thus conceived, the Prelude sets the mood for all that the music-drama is to give us of surcharged intensity and tragic power and superhuman exaltation.

But Mr. Bodanzky in *Tristan* is, at his best, more than scrupulous: he is, in this score, at his finest where the need is paramount: no one conducts the Liebestod with more profound and right an intuition of its shape and pace and texture, and all that it indicates and says. He plays it more slowly than one would have supposed it possible to do and still keep the music fluent and alive. Yet the line neither sags nor breaks. The span of the tonal arch is vast, but it soars in beauty and symmetry against the sky, and through it the wonderful music sweeps "down the long winds of ecstasy" and outward to that darkening sea of Wagner's otherworldly night.

❦ ❦ ❦

Future historians of music in America will find it difficult to believe, by the way, that one of the greatest and most famous scenes in Wagner, the unapproachable love duet (so-called) which occupies the central portion of Act II, was heard in its entirety for the first time in this country almost half a century after the music-drama was introduced here, and seventy-two years after the publication of the score. Such, however, appears to be the curious fact.

Tristan was first given in the United States at the Metropolitan Opera House, New York, December 1, 1886, and the work has since had countless representations there and at other lyric theatres in America; yet the cardinal scene in the score remained unperformed here as a whole (so far as available records show) until Leopold Stokowski, with the Philadelphia Orchestra and soloists, gave it in the course of a Wagner Festival in Philadelphia on January 15, 16, 18, 1932.[10]

Mr. Stokowski was therefore making American musical history when he performed the entire love scene of Act II (including the 400-odd measures usually elided), from the moment when

---

[10] There is a legend to the effect that that accomplished and devoted Wagnerian, Alfred Hertz, conducted an uncut presentation of *Tristan* at the Metropolitan at a special performance in March, 1909. But, although several innocent and credulous gazettes reported that *Tristan* was given on that occasion "in its entirety," as a matter of fact it was not—unhappily for some of those who were present, high-heartedly expectant.

Isolde, frantic with impatience, extinguishes the torch, while the Death motive crashes through the orchestra, to the catastrophic entrance of Mark and Melot and the courtiers as the sky turns pale above the forest trees and the lovers realize that the night of ecstasy is over and the consecrating end brought near.

No student of the score needs to be reminded of the prodigies of beauty and expressiveness contained in those seldom-heard pages restored by Stokowski. The restorations began at Tristan's "Dem Tage! dem Tage! dem tückischen Tage!" and ran to the measure before Isolde's "Doch es rächte sich der verscheuchte Tag." They comprised, further, the exquisite variations on the Peace motive—those eighty-five measures beginning at Tristan's ". . . weichen!"—thirty bars after the close of Brangäne's first song of warning from the tower, and continuing to the measure following Isolde's ". . . Tristan der Tod gegeben?"

The performance of this music under Mr. Stokowski was poetical and deeply felt. One had seldom heard a reading so full of tenderness, so responsive to the music's meaning, so affectionate and absorbed. Mr. Stokowski's tempi were often slower than tradition prescribes: but they justified themselves completely; as, for example, in the surprising beauty which he pressed from the

A-flat passage beginning at Tristan's "Was dort in keuscher Nacht," with the Night theme on the first horn: a passage that in Europe is generally taken too fast, in disregard of Wagner's instructions.

❀ ❀ ❀

It is surely an astonishing fact that *Tristan und Isolde,* one of the profoundest and longest and most exacting of lyric-dramas: a work composed by a clear-headed madman of superhuman genius, should have become, in recent years, the most popular opera in the lyric theatres of America. This does not mean that *Tristan* is now being valued for the first time in our country. In its first season at the Metropolitan, and in America, that of 1886-87, it was sung eight times by the illustrious pair of principals who introduced it here (Lilli Lehmann as Isolde and Niemann as Tristan, with Seidl conducting). What it does mean is that a great work of art is tragically dependent upon those who are its author's deputies. For such a work cannot possibly exert its full power over the mind and the imagination unless it is conveyed to us by artists of preëminent gifts. And yet we go on talking nonsense about confiding works of genius to "adequate" interpreters (heaven save the mark!), and "letting the work speak for itself"—as though, alas, it ever could!

186

What has happened to *Tristan* at the Metropolitan, and in other important theatres of America, is only that it has been wrought upon by an interpreter of genius—with electrifying results. One remembers how the most sensitive of critics defined those complementary elements that share in performances that occur when the drama becomes a rite: "the living person on the stage in whom, as before the altar, the word of the revealer is made incarnate; and the presence of the multitude silent as in its temples."

The knowing will scarcely require to be told that I refer, in the first instance, to Kirsten Flagstad, whose embodiments of Wagner's major heroines have now become an essential and necessary part of their history in America—and, indeed, a part of their effect upon their hearers. It should be borne in mind that there is nothing in the least sensational about Mme. Flagstad. She exerts none of the flashier operatic lures. She is simply an artist of insurpassable artistic devoutness and integrity who has devoted a beautiful voice, an unlapsing musical sensibility, and an imaginative insight of the rarest sort to the recreation of the masterpieces of the lyric stage. That an artist of this order, moving solely upon the most exalted planes of the musical imagination, should have attached to herself so large and fervent a public is quite as much a tribute to the taste that values her as it is to the artist herself.

And it is noteworthy that Mme. Flagstad should have won her remarkable following chiefly through her Isolde. For here, again, there is nothing sensational, no slightest overemphasis or extravagance, nothing that falls for an instant below the loftiest plane of the imagination's inner world.

It is that withdrawn world of Wagner's contemplation and intent, as he has enclosed it in the music and the poetry and the philosophy of *Tristan,* that Mme. Flagstad inhabits and illumines.

Her Isolde has preëminently that quality which marks the work of the elect interpreter: the quality of dedication, of humility and utter selflessness, in the presence of its task of re-creation. And it has that other quality which is so often the complement of the first: an art of subtle simplification and reserve, an art of exquisite and most choice economy, consorted with that translucent integrity which neither sleights nor overstresses, which gives full value to every note and word and pause, every look and every gesture— but only full value: neither more nor less.

Beyond and beside these things, this embodiment has also the mysterious rectitude of inspiration.

From the moment when this Isolde utters her significant and fateful words as she looks toward

Tristan after Brangäne parts the curtains that have closed them in, we become aware, by the subtle use of some darkening color in the voice, some strangely hieratic posture of the head, that we are confronting a figure of predestination. We know that this is the priestess and revealer, the true protagonist, of one among those few works of the creative imagination in which the central mysteries of the spirit, of love and death and destiny, are concentrated and revealed.

This artist knows that thus, and only thus, would Isolde have received the cup from the trembling Brangäne; that thus, and only thus, would she have greeted Tristan in the conniving night; that thus, and only thus, would she have stood beside his body at the end, mysteriously rapt —not an opera-singer rejoicing in a famous aria, but a figure of ecstatic reverie and transport.

Flagstad's Isolde, throughout the music's course, becomes increasingly the voice and image of Wagner's symbol of the spirit's life. The mood of consecration enwraps and appeases and exalts her. The vision of the seeress transcends even the darkening of her fallen sun; until, at the end, the unearthly beauty of the music dissolves in the transillumination of the closing page, with that ineffable ascent of the voice through the octave to the last F-sharp.

Always she is greatest when the music is greatest. The supreme thing in *Tristan* is, after all, the Liebestod; and it is in this that Mme. Flagstad is most difficult to praise sufficingly. From its opening notes she gives us its sense of mystical initiation, that liberation which is ecstasy, "the standing outside oneself in freedom," above the unrealities of a world in which she dare not stay too long. That hesitant awe, that slow and wondering consciousness of revelation, is in the music, in the gradual unfolding and expansion of the wonderful cantilena as it sounds, almost reluctantly, like a sleeper wakening, from the quiet voices of the clarinets and muted horns and muted strings. And it is reflected in the voice, the pose, the gestures of this Isolde—as she turns, for example, almost imperceptibly toward the wordless bystanders at "Seht ihr, Freunde?" as though she felt that they must share her wakening and her vision.

It is from the accretion of such moments of inspired comprehension that the great interpretation is built up, until the glory of the completed revelation irradiates the voice that soars above the climax of the orchestra, and fades from it in those last and indescribable three notes at "höchste Lust!"

❁   ❁   ❁

The lifted veil is dropped, and we are left
with only the memory of an unaccountable beauty
that has flowered and vanished in the night, and
with our endless wonder at the genius of the dead
enchanter that could give

> . . . so dread a stress
> To his cold lips, and fill with such a light
> His planetary eyes, and touch his voice
> With such a sorrow.

"*Tristan* is, and remains, a marvel to me,"
wrote Wagner candidly to the woman who had,
according to himself, inspired it: "I am more and
more unable to understand how I could produce
such a thing."

The mystery is still unsolved.

Wagner in this parable of body and soul
bent his transfiguring gaze upon the prisoning
flesh until it became as fire and air, and he beheld, instead, immortal, incandescent shapes, immortal vestures—"holy garments for glory and
for beauty."

IX

"Die Meistersinger"

WAGNER set to work upon his blithest opera, *Die Meistersinger,* during that luckless period of his middle years when his plans and hopes were crashing one by one. At Paris, in the Spring of 1861, *Tannhäuser* came to grief. His efforts to get *Tristan* staged at the Vienna Opera were fruitless. The *Ring,* unfinished and abandoned, lay silent on his shelf. His existence became a long and cumulative nightmare. He had written all his works save *Die Meistersinger,* part of the *Ring,* and *Parsifal.* Yet he could say with truth, as well as with bitterness, what he wrote in September, 1863, in his fifty-first year, to Editha von Rhaden: "After my death, those who survey my life's vicissitudes will be amazed that a creative artist like myself, whose works were warmly received in many quarters during his lifetime, could nevertheless not get sufficient support from his contemporaries even to create." The greatest musician since Beethoven pleaded in vain with his publishers and potential backers to provide him with a livelihood so that he might secure the necessary peace and leisure for his uncompleted work, and not waste his priceless time and strength upon the giving of concerts in order to obtain the wherewithal to live. Later, after he had fled from his creditors in Vienna, he wrote despairingly to his friend and disciple, Peter Cornelius, that he had come to feel that every hope was vain. "My situation is perilous; I balance on the narrowest foothold—one push and all is over: there will be nothing more to be got out of me then, nothing, nothing more! *Some* light must show itself, *someone* must arise to give me vigorous help! . . . But perhaps it is all no use now! Indeed, I feel within me that the end approaches. Ill-health does its worst to rivet this mood. . . . Some benevolent saving miracle must come to me, otherwise all is over!"

Yet, in the midst of this progressive blackening of his skies, tormented by illness, anxiety, difficulties of every sort, and, toward the last, with anguish and hopelessness and the conviction of approaching death, he had been setting down on paper, in spite of harassing interruptions,[1] the wisest, sanest, and serenest music that ever was poured out by the creative mind of man: music in

---

[1] Wagner wrote to his publisher, Schott, from Vienna, on September 12, 1863, that "nearly one hundred pages of script of the score, in very small writing, are already finished, and I could let you have these now." He wrote on April 25, 1864, that "the principal part of the whole [opera] is sketched."

which the quintessence of poised and lovely and humorous benignity is distilled.

But even after his dramatic rescue by King Ludwig, the composition of *Die Meistersinger* did not proceed uninterruptedly to its end. The great adventure with Cosima began; the production of *Tristan* supervened. And then, at last, in the relative quiet of his retreat at Triebschen, in his fifty-fifth year, with Cosima to guard and solace and sustain him, *Die Meistersinger* was completed. The autograph score bears the annotation: "Ende der Triebschen, Donnerstag, 24 Okt. 1867, Abends 8 Uhr, R.W." [2]

❦   ❦   ❦

Die Meistersinger, like Wagner's other greater works, had what Emerson would have called "a long foreground." Wagner sketched the plan of the comedy in 1845, in his thirty-third year, shortly after he had finished *Tannhäuser;* and its earliest draft was coeval with that of *Lohengrin.* It was a result of that same Marienbad holiday to which allusion was made in an earlier chapter of this book.[3]

Wagner in his Autobiography [4] has left us

---

[2] The first performance of *Die Meistersinger* was at Munich, June 21, 1868, under Hans von Bülow.

[3] Pages 59-60.

[4] *Mein Leben,* by Richard Wagner. Munich: F. Bruckmann, Ltd., 1911; New York: Dodd, Mead & Co., 1911.

a characteristic account of the opera's inception. In that Summer of 1845, between the completion and production of *Tannhäuser,* he started on a holiday, "which consisted," he wrote, "of a journey to Marienbad in Bohemia, where my wife and I intended to take the 'cure.' It was a marvellous Summer, almost too hot, and I was therefore in high spirits. I had intended to follow the easygoing mode of life which is a necessary part of that somewhat trying treatment, and had brought along some books with me—the poems of Wolfram von Eschenbach, as well as the anonymous epic, *Lohengrin.*"

But an "easy-going mode of life" was scarcely possible for Wagner. Before he knew it, while he was secluding himself at Marienbad in the neighboring pine woods of that delectable resort, re-creating one of those legendary worlds in which he loved to dwell, "in company with Titurel and Parsifal," as he tells us, he found himself returning to the thought of his plan for an opera on the subject of Lohengrin. The result, he says, was an ever-increasing state of excitement. He remembered his doctor's advice to relax. His relaxation took the form of working out a scheme for a comedy on the subject of the Mastersingers of Nuremberg. He had read in Gervinus's History of German Literature references to the Nuremberg Mastersingers, with Hans Sachs as

195

the chief figure, which acquired, he says, "a vital charm" for him. The "Marker" (Beckmesser in the completed opera), and his function in the Guild, especially pleased him; and there came to him, on one of his solitary walks, "the idea of a humorous scene in which the cobbler, as a popular artisan poet, should seek revenge on the pedantic Marker by giving him a practical lesson in singing." The scene was to culminate when the Marker exhibited his slate covered with accusing chalk-marks, while Hans Sachs displayed his finished shoes (this idea furnished eventually two different scenes in *Die Meistersinger*). "To this scene," says Wagner, "by way of concluding the Second Act, I added a scene consisting of a narrow, crooked street in medieval Nuremberg, with crowds of excited neighbors, ultimately engaging in a street riot." [5] The conception produced so vivid a picture in his imagination that, as he says, "the whole of my *Meistersinger* comedy took shape before me. Inasmuch as it was a particularly cheerful subject, and not in the least likely to overexcite my nerves, I felt I must write

[5] This scene had its origin in an actual experience of Wagner's at Nuremberg years earlier, during his Magdeburg conductorship, when he was a witness one night of just such a scene of tumult, with the narrow streets filled by an excited crowd, which melted away as suddenly as it had gathered—whereupon Wagner and his companion, as he tells us, "were able to stroll home through the moonlit streets, quietly jesting and laughing." He describes the incident at length in *Mein Leben*.

it out in spite of the doctor's orders. I therefore proceeded to do this, and hoped it might free me from the thralldom of the idea of *Lohengrin*. But I was mistaken. . . ."

Wagner drafted at that time the first prose sketch for the libretto of what was to become, twenty-two years later, his comedy in music, *Die Meistersinger*. This early sketch, and two later ones of 1861, may be read in the complete German edition of Wagner's Collected Works. In the second and third prose-drafts, written at Vienna in 1861, the character of the bigoted Marker is named "Hanslich," and was obviously intended as a satirical caricature of Wagner's critical adversary, the Viennese anti-Wagnerite, Eduard Hanslick.[6] But Wagner was too wise and sensitive an artist not to realize the aesthetic error of so crass a kind of satire; and in *Die Meistersinger*, as it was completed, the pedantic and obscurantist Marker became "Beckmesser" (the name of one of the historic Mastersingers of Nuremberg).

Wagner's intention, in 1845, of writing a comic opera "as soon as he could set about it" was strengthened, he says, "by the well-meant advice of good friends who wished me to compose an opera of 'lighter character,' since they believed

[6] Eduard Hanslick, an influential Viennese music critic and writer on aesthetics, was born at Prague, September 11, 1825, and died at Baden, near Vienna, August 6, 1904.

that such a work would open the doors of most German theatres to me, and thus effect a beneficial change in my outward circumstances, which had begun to assume a threatening aspect. With the Athenians, a jovial Satyr-play was wont to follow the Tragedy; so, during that Marienbad holiday, I conceived the idea of a comic piece which might well form a Satyr-play as pendant to the tragedy of *Tannhäuser*. This was *Die Meistersinger von Nürnberg*."

❦ ❦ ❦

As it turned out, the *Meistersinger* project remained dormant in his mind for sixteen years. When he finally took it up again, in 1861, he was actuated by virtually the same reason which, he says, "strengthened his original intention." "My wish to apply myself to some easier, less exhausting, and speedier work," he wrote the music publisher Schott of Mainz, on October 30th of that year, "is reinforced by consideration of the difficulties with which I have to contend in getting my serious works performed . . . I long to undertake some kind of artistic activity which would occupy me pleasantly and distract my mind. At this time and to this end I do not feel that I can return to my great *Nibelung* work [of which, it will be remembered, only *Das Rheingold, Die Walküre,* and the first two Acts of *Siegfried* had thus far been composed] . . . I believe it is a happy thought, according with my mood and circumstances, to put in hand at once the execution of an earlier idea for a popular operatic comedy. The opera is called *Die Meistersinger von Nürnberg,* and the chief hero is the jovial poet Hans Sachs . . . The style in poetry and music shall be thoroughly light and popular. A rapid circulation through all theatres may be anticipated, since this time I shall need neither a so-called 'first tenor' nor a great tragic soprano."

As in the case of *Tristan*—which also had been undertaken as something popular, easy, and available—he does not seem to have realized how great a thing he was about to produce.

He writes Schott from Vienna on November 20, 1861, that he has just dispatched to him "the finished sketch for a great comic opera. You will see the kind of thing it is, and will no doubt agree that I am right in forecasting it as one of my most original and popular works. I have been saving up this cheerful piece of work for a long time . . ." He assures the publisher that in *Die Meistersinger* he "does not in the least intend to offer unworthy work." The subject permits him to write "clear, transparent, yet pithy music in the gayest colors."

Wagner proposed to deliver the finished

poem of the comedy on January 1, 1862; but already, according to his habit, the music had begun to germinate in his mind. In November he had paid a visit to his former "Muse," Mathilde Wesendonck, and her husband, who were in Venice; and it was then that he appears to have arrived at one of his earliest musical crystallizations of the *Meistersinger* subject.

That visit to the Wesendoncks must have been a bit trying, and Wagner writes of it in his Autobiography with more than a touch of bitterness (it should be remembered that the Zürich catastrophe [7] was only a little more than three years behind him). Poor Wesendonck evidently succeeded in getting on Wagner's nerves. "My friends," he tells us, "were in very flourishing circumstances, and . . . fully expected that my participation in their enjoyment would drive away my blues. They seemed to have no wish to realize my position . . ." Otto Wesendonck went about armed with huge field-glasses for sightseeing, and only once, says Wagner, "took me with him to see the Academy of Arts, which I had known from the outside only."

Wagner's despondency, however, was somewhat relieved by a mystically kindling experience that he records in his Autobiography. Gazing upon Titian's painting of the Assumption of the

[7] See the preceding chapter on *Tristan und Isolde*.

Virgin, he found that it "exercised a most sublime influence" upon him. "As soon as I realized its conception," he says, "my old powers revived in me, as though by a sudden flash of inspiration. I determined at once to get to work upon *Die Meistersinger!*" After spending "four dreary days" in Venice, he returned to Vienna on November 13th, and, he says, "it was during this journey that the music of *Die Meistersinger* first dawned on my mind, in which I still retained the scenario as I had originally drafted it [at Marienbad sixteen years before]. With the utmost distinctness I at once conceived the principal part of the Prelude in C major. Under the influence of these impressions, I arrived in Vienna in a very cheerful frame of mind. I at once announced my return to Cornelius. . . . The communication of my plan for the immediate resumption of my work on *Die Meistersinger* made him almost frantic with delight, and until my departure from Vienna he remained in a state of delirious excitement."

Cornelius undertook to provide Wagner with the necessary data for his comedy. "I made a careful study," says Wagner, "of Grimm's controversial essay on the Songs of the Mastersingers; then it became necessary for me to procure the Nuremberg Chronicle of old Wagenseil from the Imperial Library." It was from Wagen-

seil's Chronicle [8] that Wagner derived most of the
data that enabled him to give *Die Meistersinger*
its marvellous verisimilitude—that, and his own
unfailing genius for imaginative re-creation.

Wagner, provided with this invaluable
source-book, went to Paris in the Winter of 1861-
62, and took a small room on the Quai Voltaire.
"I often laugh out loud," he wrote to Mathilde
Wesendonck on December 21st, "when I raise my
eyes from my work and see through my window
the Tuileries and Louvre straight opposite; for
you must know that my real self is now roaming
the streets of Nuremberg, and mixing with somewhat blunt, square-cornered folk." He tells us
that while strolling through the galleries of the
Palais Royal on the way to the Taverne Anglaise,
he conceived the melody of the great chorale,
"Wach' Auf," with which the populace in the last
Act of *Die Meistersinger* greet their beloved
master Hans Sachs.

[8] Johann Christoph Wagenseil, Doctor and Professor of Law,
was born at Nuremberg in 1633 (seventy-three years after the
period of *Die Meistersinger*) and died at Altdorf in 1708. His
book is an invaluable account of the City of Nuremberg, its affairs
and institutions, with illustrations of the city as it looked in the
seventeenth century. An Appendix to Wagenseil's book is entitled:
*Johann Christof Wagenseil's Book of the Master-singers' Gracious
Art; Its Origin, Practice, Utility and Rules.* And there are detailed accounts of the "Complete Tabulatur [the rules of prosody,
and the like, observed by the Mastersingers]," and of "The
Master-singers' Manners and Customs at the Singing-School and
in Convivial Meetings."

By the close of the year, it seems to have dawned on him that the new work was turning out to be something rather different from what he had expected. Writing to Mathilde Wesendonck from Paris at the end of December, he says:

"I shall often send you a morsel from my work. How you will open your eyes over my *Meistersinger!* Fortify your heart against Sachs —you will fall in love with him! It is a really wonderful work. The old draft afforded little— next to nothing. Yes, one must oneself have been in Paradise in order to find one's way at length to the heart of such a subject!"

On January 17, 1862, he writes Schott that he hopes in a fortnight's time to have the libretto ready for composition, and to read him the whole work—"which when finished takes on an aspect very different from that of the faint indications of a first rough sketch. The music is already complete in my brain"—a noteworthy statement, especially as he wrote to Malwida von Meysenbug, from Biebrich, two months later (March 12th), that, having "written the whole poem of *Die Meistersinger* in a month," finishing it by the end of January, "the next thing was to find a refuge where I could write music for it. I have achieved this at last, here in Biebrich . . . Tomorrow I hope to begin composition."

He had settled at Biebrich, in February,
1862, in "a couple of nice rooms, magnificently
situated on the brink of the Rhine." On March
12th he wrote Mathilde that he hoped "to start
work at last tomorrow . . . I am thoroughly
settled here now, have two chambers hired for a
year, the pianoforte, bookcase, renowned divan,
the three Roman engravings and the old Nibelungen print . . . The site is extraordinarily
lovely . . . There is a beautiful, quite spacious
garden; the birds in the Duke's park keep up a
contest of song with those on the island opposite;
the nightingales are numberless, they say, and
positively deafening in their season. So here will
I await my *Meistersinger* destiny . . ."

"The fair season of the year," he says in his
Autobiography, "was now approaching, and I
was once more seized with a desire for work. As
from the balcony of my flat, in a sunset of great
splendor, I gazed upon the magnificent spectacle
of 'Golden' Mayence, with the majestic Rhine
pouring along its outskirts in a glory of light, the
Prelude to my *Meistersinger* again suddenly made
its presence closely and distinctly felt in my soul.
Once before [on the train journey from Venice
to Vienna, in the previous November] had I seen
it rise before me out of a lake of sorrow, like some
distant mirage. I proceeded to write down the
Prelude exactly as it appears today in the score,

containing the clear outlines of the leading themes of the whole drama.[9]

By May 22nd—his forty-ninth birthday—he had reached a point where he found it possible to say to the Countess Pourtalès concerning his evolving masterpiece—that work which was intended to be "thoroughly light and popular": "I see clearly, and with certainty, that this is my greatest achievement. When some day you hear the Prelude to the Third Act (I often depart from serial order as I work), and then the chorus with which the people enthusiastically receive Hans Sachs . . . be sure you remember what frame of mind I was in on this birthday of mine."

❧ ❧ ❧

A great musician, who is also a great man, one whose culture is as liberal and seasoned as his wisdom is profound,—Ignace Paderewski,—has been quoted as saying that he considers *Die Meistersinger* not only "the greatest work of genius ever achieved by a musician, but the greatest ever achieved by any artist in any field of human activity." This is a daring opinion, mag-

---

[9] In the following Autumn (November 1, 1862), Wagner conducted the Prelude at a specially organized concert in the Gewandhaus at Leipzig. The audience was small, but so responsive that the Prelude was at once repeated. The discerning critic of the *Signale,* discussing the new work, did not, however, share the public's enthusiasm. He characterized the Prelude as "a chaos, a 'tohu-wabohu' [*sic*], and nothing more."

nificently unqualified. Perhaps it is overgenerous
—though that need not be insisted upon by those
of us who happen to care for *Die Meistersinger*
with the special affection felt by most Wagnerians
for that work. Yet it may be said that there are
many musicians who are likewise convinced of
the preëminence of Wagner's compendious and
magical score. What, as a matter of fact, can one
set beside it?

The arguments which Mr. Paderewski might
have advanced in support of his opinion are many,
and some of them are not difficult to imagine.

The music of *Die Meistersinger* flows from
a seemingly inexhaustible spring of pure and
lovely and characteristic song. Here, surely, are
the most endearing tunes, the loveliest and
strongest and most salient, that ever welled from
a musician's brain. Here, in this huge and prodigal score, is—as John Runciman said—"the
longest song in existence." And what a song! A
song in praise of song—the very spirit of lyric
beauty exalting itself by its own rhapsodic praise.
And consider that this mighty burgeoning of
song, this matchless blossoming, is evolved and
patterned with a mastery that never fails. For
hour after hour the music flowers inexhaustibly,
song upon song, as if the creative spirit and the
shaping will were inexhaustible in fertility and
strength.

It is music at once profound and blithe, tranquil and poignant, homespun and magical. For in this huge and bountiful score, tragedy is masked by a deep and comprehending magnanimity that fills up all one's sense of the greatness of the human spirit.

Perhaps the most singular of all the critical oddities provoked by Wagner was uttered by a foreign writer, who observed not long ago that "the dramatic business of *Die Meistersinger* is a slight, sentimental comedy, a pint-pot-comedy"— this of a drama whose action is almost as interior as that of *Tristan und Isolde!* For the essential drama of *Die Meistersinger* is played in the soul of Hans Sachs; and Sachs, for all his homely humor and his bonhomie, is at bottom a figure of tragedy.

The real Hans Sachs [10] married twice and

[10] The historic Hans Sachs—"whose memory will be revered by the folk," says a contemporary eulogist, "so long as the world standeth, no less than those of Homer, Virgil, Ovid, and Horace by the learned"—was born at Nuremberg in 1494, and died in 1576. His first wife died on March 18, 1560, and he married her successor on September 2, 1561, when he was sixty-six. When one remembers that Sachs is represented as a widower in Wagner's opera, it becomes apparent to the mathematically minded that that eventful Midsummer Day must have fallen either in June, 1560 (three months after Sachs' first wife died), or in June, 1561 (two and a half months before he married again). This "patriarch of the Master-singers," as old Wagenseil calls him, "brought their art into such vogue that in his time over 250 Master-singers existed in Nuremberg." Sachs' own master-songs, says Wagenseil, "show much invention, and are so discreetly handled that at that time

lived to be over eighty-one, so that he was able to write (as Wagenseil assures us) 4,370 master-songs. Wagner's Sachs, a widower, took no second wife. Instead, he took renunciation for his bride; and his noblest master-song was the deep and exquisite music of resignation and serene content that issues from this most wonderful of comedies. The historic Sachs has been turned into a unique creation by the genius of Wagner. It is he, not Walther, not the Folk, who is the real hero of the tragi-comedy. What a character Wagner has given us here!—this poet, dreamer, man of sorrows: this tragedian who has mastered his grief and does not take too seriously his resignation; who is mellow without softness, noble without offensiveness. The Sachs of Wagner's imagination is, in those intenser moments when he confronts his own heart, the man of Hardy's terrible poem, *I Look Into My Glass:* the middle-aged lover with his wintering body shaken in the evening of its days "with throbbings of noontide."

Like all true humorists, he is tolerant, philosophic. He is a man of infinite charm—magnetic, dominant, lovable; fine-fibred yet homespun; a being of fathomless tenderness, yet one who

they could not well have been better, and by reason of their splendid vigor and good sense, are much to be preferred to what has been written of late."

"holds a birchrod over sentimentalism"; a liberal and a modernist, yet a lover of that which is abiding in the past.

Observe him at that moment in the Third Act when his self-control is most difficult—when Eva throws herself into his arms and unknowingly torments him with her gratitude that she swears is love. Here, for an instant, we see the anguished, middle-aged lover of Wagner's piercing conception, with his sorrow, his fortitude, his resignation, his magnitude of soul; and, later, his quiet acceptance of his own tragedy, his tenderness that is never for himself.

It is this element in *Die Meistersinger* which makes it so much more moving and profound a thing than many have supposed it to be. It has been called "a work full of health, fun, and happiness" (which, to be sure, it is, externally), containing "not a single bar of love music that can be described as passionate." If by this is meant that the love music of Walther and Eva and the poignant brooding of Sachs are in a different world from the love music of *Tristan und Isolde,* that is, of course, as true as it is obvious—and was scarcely worth remarking.

What specially distinguishes *Die Meistersinger* is the completeness with which it illustrates the ability of first-rate creative minds to give a universal implication and significance to the localized and the particular. The miracle that Wagner achieves in *Die Meistersinger* is at the opposite pole from that contrary miracle which he achieves in *Tristan,* for example.

In *Tristan,* he works inward from the generalized to the particular: he takes those vast and immemorial patterns of desire and grief, sorrow and despair and ecstasy, and makes them personal and intimate to ourselves, so that this timeless world of love and death becomes for us the familiar meeting-place of little lives.

In *Die Meistersinger,* he shows us that contrary miracle of great art: he shows us how, at the releasing touch of an imagination universal in sympathy and scope, the particular becomes the generalized, the parish becomes the world.

"My real self," I have quoted Wagner as writing to Mathilde Wesendonck from Paris as he worked on the score, "is roaming the streets of Nuremberg and mixing with somewhat blunt, square-cornered folk." In sixteenth-century Nuremberg he had walked and slept and dreamt indeed! Was ever a work of art more deeply tinctured with the particular? Was ever an opera more parochial than this living re-creation of medieval Nuremberg, "with its thousand gable-ends, its fragrant lime-trees and gardens, its ancient customs, its processions of the guilds and crafts, its watchman with his horn and lantern, calling the hour, its freshness and quaint loveliness by day and its sweetness on soft summer nights"?

By what feat of transmutation has that vanished time, that vanished life, been made to seem so near and so accessible to us of a twentieth-century day, alien and new and harshly bright? Why do the watchman with his horn, the gabled, moonlit houses, the old and narrow streets, the roistering apprentices, the thronging, processional Guilds, fit so gratefully into the patterns of our delighted minds as we sit before this magically recaptured world?

Is it because, despite the individualized and concrete limning of characters and scenes, the rich, exact veracity of the portraiture that makes *Die Meistersinger* so astonishing an achievement, Wagner could not, even here, overcome his propensity for dealing with everlasting things? Writing to Otto Wesendonck during the composition of *Die Meistersinger,* and referring to the character of Pogner, Wagner declared: "I really feel that I have built a monument to a friend in the love with which I have handled this part." But indeed he is constantly memorializing throughout *Die Meistersinger*. Pogner, and Hans Sachs, and Eva, and Walther, and Beckmesser, are all, at bottom, prototypes, warm and living symbolizations. In their habits walk Abundance and Gener-

osity and Benignity and Romantic Youth and
Malice (since there must be a villain, even if he
be only an absurd one, in even the loveliest of
fables).

🏵   🏵   🏵

No one has written with truer insight into
the special quality of *Die Meistersinger* than
Cosima Wagner, a critic of remarkable sensibility
and penetration. The comments upon the work
that she confided to her letters while *Die Meistersinger* went forward to completion, in the early
sixties, and later at Triebschen, are as treasurable
as they are little known.

At Biebrich, in 1862, before she joined her
fortunes with Wagner's, she had her earliest
knowledge of the work, and wrote of it thus to her
friend Meissner: "Like Shakespeare, Wagner has
effected a unity between comedy and the sublime. Greatness hangs like a sun over the plot, in
which humor is combined with the profoundest
emotion." Writing to her father, Liszt, at the
same period, she was more expansive: *"Die
Meistersinger,"* she declared, "is to Wagner's
creations what *The Winter's Tale* is to Shakespeare's other works. Wagner's imagination has
made an excursion into realms of mischievous
gaiety, and has so conjured up medieval Nuremberg, with its guilds and corporations, its crafts-
men-poets, its pedants, and its knights, as to call

forth in the sublimest and most noble way the laughter that does most to emancipate the spirit. Quite apart from the intellectual content and import of the work, its artistic execution may be compared with the tabernacle in the Church of St. Lawrence [at Nuremberg]. Like the sculptor of the tabernacle, the musician has here achieved the purest and most graceful form, with the most consummate boldness of conception; and just as, at the base of the tabernacle, Adam Krafft bears up and supports the whole structure with an expression of grave and concentrated reverence, so in *Die Meistersinger* it is the figure of Hans Sachs that dominates and directs the action with a cheerful and lovable serenity."

Early in 1867, she wrote to King Ludwig: "If only I could send you the wondrous music that I am hearing! It is like a deep, musical radiance. In this sunlit transport one does not know whether one is listening to light or seeing sound —it is as though the old houses themselves were moving off in solemn procession . . ."

❁　❁　❁

For some, this is the most endearing of all scores; and deep is the happiness of those who are so fortunate as to hear it revealingly performed —as, at the Metropolitan, with the sage and mellowed and glowing Sachs of Mr. Schorr:

probably the finest embodiment of the character that is now to be seen in any lyric theatre. Here, unmistakably, is the figure of Wagner's play and music—the poet, the dreamer, the tragedian with a sense of humor. No one in our time has delivered so admirably that Second-Act monologue, "Was duftet doch der Flieder," in which the music permits us to look, for the first time, into the spirit and the mind of Sachs, that music which must always be the despair of any artist who is not at once an instinctive poet and a master of song. And how persuasively Mr. Schorr can make himself the visual image of Wagner's tragic comedian as one's imagination sees him!—an image that might have stepped from a canvas by Holbein.   ❧   ❧   ❧

The great, golden laughter that Wagner releases in *Die Meistersinger* is a thing apart. So, too, is its enamoring blend of poetry and humor —Shakespearean magic in a dimension that Shakespeare did not know. At the close of the Second Act, as the rioters disperse and the tumult dies down, and the doors are closed and the lights put out, leaving the stage quite empty and still and dark, the Night Watchman arrives on the scene with his lantern and his ox-horn, rubbing his eyes, singing his quavering call, and we see the moon rise above old Nuremberg sleeping in the heart of a forgotten but recovered century, while the murmuring orchestra reminds us of the brooding enchantment of the Summer night. Then, once again, we realize that there is nothing in music to set beside this lovable masterwork, with its beauty and serene philosophy, its delicate, exact recapturing of the hue and fragrance of a vanished day, its perfect veracity and transcendent art.

This utterance of a rich and tranquil spirit, so warm and humorous and so deeply wise, must remain among those things which live for the unfailing reassurance of the minds of men.

X

"Parsifal"

A<small>LONE</small> among Wagner's works, *Parsifal* is in
need of repeated validation. For this profound and mystical drama, in which the most passionate and despotic artist in the history of music
speaks to us so gravely and loftily and tenderly
of quiet things—of mercy and understanding, and
the beauty of compassion, and the wisdom of the
pure in heart: this anomalous product is alien to
the sympathies and tastes of many.

The work, undoubtedly, raises its own
barriers for the impatient and the undiscerning.
We have ever with us those unduly contemptuous
music lovers and musicians who look askance at
Parsifal because of the fact that many devout
and simple souls who can hardly be suspected of
musical discernment regard attendance upon it as
an exercise in piety. We have always with us, too,
those who profess to be indignant because of its
alleged exploitation of holy things; and there are
other and implacable objectors who sincerely
loathe the work not because it is an "exploitation"
of holy things, but because it deals with holy
things at all—yet there are complete and perfect

infidels who are known to admire Hubert van
Eyck's Three Marys at the Sepulchre, and the
Cathedral at Chartres, and the *St. Matthew
Passion.*

Schuré once remarked that the anomaly of
such a phenomenon as Wagner in his own day
was "an event in itself," and that Wagner felt
compelled from time to time to clear up the mis-
understandings existing between himself and the
world by a manifesto: "But the more he explained, the deeper the gulf became. The theatre
as Wagner conceived it was a temple, whereas
the theatre of his day was a booth or a fair. He
spoke the language of priests, yet shopkeepers
were expected to understand him."

The misunderstanding persists, half a
century after Wagner's death; and we may witness today the grotesque spectacle of publics less
enlightened and receptive than our own attempt-
ing to adjust such works as *Tristan* and *Götterdämmerung* and *Parsifal* to environments in
which they have no place.

"All Art," says Gilbert Murray in the preface to his translation of the *Agamemnon,* "moves
in its course of development from Religion to
Entertainment, from a Service to a Performance." It was one of the most signal of Wagner's
achievements that, so far as his own greater
works could serve as examples, they tended to re-

217

verse that process of trivialization and debasement. His designation of *Parsifal* points this distinction, and is highly significant. He does not call the work an "opera," or a "lyric-drama," or a "music-drama," or—as he called *Der Ring des Nibelungen*—a "festival drama": he calls it "a sacred festival play," or "stage-consecrating festival drama."

Since he was not only an idealist and a mystic, but the sagest and most tough-minded of realists, Wagner was well aware of what he described as "the madness of the attempt" to take an institution, the operatic theatre of his day, "whose public function was almost exclusively devoted to the distraction and amusement of people bored to death by pleasure, and employ it for a diametrically opposite purpose: namely, the abstraction of its public from their everyday interest for the purpose of attuning them to a reverent reception of the loftiest and sincerest things the human mind can grasp. . . ." "History," he continued,[1] "supplied me with a model for that ideal relation between the theatre and its public of which I had dreamt. I found it in the theatre of ancient Athens, where its walls were thrown open on none but special, sacred feast-days; where the taste for Art was coupled with the celebration of a religious rite . . . in which the most illustrious

---

[1] *Zukunftsmusik* (1860).

members of the State themselves took part as poets and performers, to appear like priests before . . . a public filled with such exalted expectations of the sublimity of the conceptions to be set before them, that a Sophocles, an Aeschylus, could express the deepest meanings of all poems, assured of their understanding by the populace."

Those convictions regarding the function of the stage as Wagner conceived it in relation to the communal life apply not only to works of such special character as the *Ring* and *Parsifal,* but, in varying degree, to all his works after *Rienzi.*

"The life of art," wrote the inimitable Stark Young, "is entertainment." No doubt, in the true and deeper sense in which he meant it, *Hamlet* is entertaining, as well as Mr. Ed Wynn; and in this profounder conception of the term, *Tristan* and *Götterdämmerung* and *Parsifal,* too, are entertaining—in the sense that they "take you, draw you on, fill you with their essence: substitute, temporarily, their own life for your own." But in the casual and ordinary sense of the word, the later works of Wagner are incompletely entertaining. They are works of unique earnestness, conceived with no thought of the preferences and requirements of the average listener. Their uncompromising seriousness, their immensity of dramatic, philosophical, and musical design, their tyrannical drafts upon the comprehension and staying-power of an audience, make any comparison between them and the average opera ridiculous; and of all Wagner's dramas, *Parsifal* is least adapted to any but a special and qualified public.

It is astonishing, when one stops to think of it, that *Parsifal* should have survived into the third decade of the twentieth century. What extremity of contempt and abuse has not been poured upon it! Between those who disapprove of *Parsifal* because, as they have thought and said, it makes capital of sacred things, and those who object to it because it deals with sacred things at all, Wagner's much-enduring *Bühnenweihfestspiel* has been sadly buffeted. As if this were not enough, the work has had to endure attacks from other quarters. There have been defenders of the hearth and home who, with an ingenuity worthy of a better cause, have discovered a taint of "immorality" in *Parsifal*—though, oddly enough, as Ernest Newman once remarked, "during the last thirty years [it is more than half a century now], millions of human beings have been moved by *Parsifal* as they have never been moved by any other work in any art. For the vast majority of us, it breathes the purest spiritual aspiration that the human soul has ever found voice for."

"Guileless innocents!" you can imagine the

detractors of *Parsifal* retorting, in a withering unison of contempt.

Finally, there are those for whom *Parsifal,* considered solely as music, is an inferior product of the Wagnerian Muse—"the last sad quaverings of a beloved friend," as John Runciman, I think, once called it.

And yet, *Parsifal* endures—a monumental anachronism in our half-skeptical, half-bigoted age. Even in an environment far removed from the setting that Wagner specifically designed for it—even in New York, with Broadway outside the door—*Parsifal* survives. With more than a generation of performances behind it, *Parsifal* attracts today a larger and more obviously musical audience than it ever did. It is an audience that listens with unbroken quiet and absorption during the progress of the formidable work: an audience whose reverential attitude is not one of conventional piety in the presence of religious symbols and evocations, but of spontaneous response to the disclosure of a beauty so conquering and transcendent that even the rationalist is sometimes wordless in its presence. Year after year the Metropolitan's *Parsifal* audience passes silently from the auditorium as the curtains close upon that scene which none but Wagner could have made so lasting a possession of our inner world: the Glorification in the Temple, with its gold and crimson and blue and silver lights, its hovering, luminous dove, the consecrated Parsifal and the refulgent Grail, and the worshipping knights, and Wagner's unearthly music.

❦　　❦　　❦

Nevertheless, the realistic observer is aware of a maladjustment in the relation between *Parsifal* and many sophisticated music lovers and musicians. But this need not disturb him. A wise observer remarked not long ago, in discussing the mystery of man's relation to the universe, that "great values and ideals retain their greatness and derive their interest and force from their position *sub specie æternitatis.*" But one likes to think that the speaker would also have pointed out, had he been discussing not life alone but the expressions of life, that "art is not an entity: it is a type of organization . . . The nature of living things is determined, not by the nature of their parts, but by the nature or principle of their organization." Art has no eternal verities save those that are constituted by its truth to its own expressional intention, and the fidelity with which it achieves its imaginative mastery of its material. The imagination, said Keats, is not a state: it is existence itself.

Thus we see that *Parsifal* is neither validated nor invalidated by its supposed "system of ethics,"

222

by its persuasiveness or its alleged absurdity as a
spiritual fable. It prevails, for those who are concerned with essentials, because it is the ripened
issue of a great mind's long and searching contact with existence; and because that issue of reflection and experience has been transvalued and
shaped and organized by a supreme artist's
mastery of articulate design. In other words, it
prevails, simply and sufficiently, because of the
integrity and the power of the creative mind
which generated its imaginative content and organized its presented form.

❀   ❀   ❀

For more than half his lifetime, with varying intentness and continuity, Wagner was concerned with the idea of *Parsifal*.

As early as 1845, at Marienbad—when, as
we have seen in the preceding chapter, he occupied himself not only with his *Lohengrin* project,
but with the plan for an opera about the Master-
singers of Nuremberg—he read the Parsifal epic
of Wolfram von Eschenbach. "With my book
under my arm," he says in his Autobiography, "I
hid myself in the neighboring woods, and pitch-
ing my tent by the brook in company with Titurel
and Parsifal, I lost myself in Wolfram's strange
yet irresistibly charming poem." Thereafter, the
basic conceptions that were later to find complete

223

expression in *Parsifal* were seldom absent from his thoughts and plans. There are elements of the future *Parsifal* not only in *Lohengrin,* but in two projects which Wagner never brought to fulfillment: the five-act drama, *Jesus of Nazareth,* which he sketched in 1848; and the Buddhistic *Die Sieger,* which he worked upon eight years later.

The earliest sketch of the *Parsifal* drama appears to date from the *Tristan* period. At Zürich, in the Spring of 1857,[2] Wagner, on Good Friday, "in an hour of deep poetic reverie," recalled the incident of Parsifal's encounter with the pilgrims on that holy day, as related by Chrétien de Troyes and Wolfram von Eschenbach; and thereupon he drafted a rough sketch of what was to become, twenty years later, the drama of *Parsifal,* with its central idea of compassion as the loftiest of spiritual motives, and its central figure of the stainless

[2] Some of Wagner's biographers (the late William Ashton Ellis among them) have conjectured that Wagner was in error when he wrote in *Mein Leben* that he sketched the *Parsifal* drama at Zürich in 1857. Mr. Ellis believed that Wagner's memory slipped, and that the year was 1858, not 1857. I am informed, however, by Dr. Otto Strobel, curator of Wagner's manuscripts in the archives at Bayreuth, that the sketch of the *Parsifal* drama was, as Wagner said, begun on Good Friday, April 10, 1857—*not* 1858; though Wagner was mistaken in thinking that he had, on that date, already moved into the Asyl, the cottage on the Wesendonck estate occupied by himself and Minna. The supposition, long popular with earlier historians, that the music of the Good Friday scene in *Parsifal,* as well as the sketch of the drama, dates from 1857, is, according to Dr. Strobel, unfounded.

and enlightened redeemer, who conquered through pity and renunciation.

In August, 1865, he made a more elaborate sketch of the drama for King Ludwig II. But it was not until *Die Meistersinger* and the *Ring* had been produced that he completed, in 1877, the text of the dramatic poem, which was published at the end of the year. He began work on the music in the same year. The Prelude was sketched by September 27, 1877. The first performance of the completed Prelude was a private one, at Wahnfried, Bayreuth, on December 25, 1878, the birthday of Cosima. It was played on that occasion by the Meiningen Court Orchestra, with Wagner conducting. The composition of the music-drama was finished on April 26, 1879, and the instrumentation on January 13, 1882, at Palermo— though the autograph score is dated "December 25, 1881." [3] The first performance of *Parsifal* in

[3] The actual date of the completion of Wagner's last music-drama involved an amiable deception on his part. He wanted to present the finished manuscript of the orchestral score to Cosima as a gift for her forty-fourth birthday, which fell on Christmas, 1881; but he found himself unable to complete the instrumentation of the last Act on time—twenty-three pages of the final scene remained to be orchestrated to his satisfaction. So, anxious to carry out his plans, he perpetrated what Cosima afterward described as a "pious fraud": he orchestrated the last page, and on Christmas morning laid the score on Cosima's gift-table with that page upward (and the uncompleted pages hidden), inscribing it, "für dich!—25th Dez., 1881. R.W." The score was not finished until nineteen days later. But the other date still stands in the manuscript.

225

its entirety was at the Festspielhaus, Bayreuth, July 26, 1882, under the direction of Hermann Levi.[4]

❦   ❦   ❦

Each of Wagner's essays in musico-dramatic symbolism is based on some phase of the conscious or unconscious human struggle toward spiritual achievement and perfection. It is evident that his works are connected by a philosophical and symbolistic thread that was always present in his own mind, even though it is not invariably clear to ours. His Prose Works and his Correspondence leave us in no doubt of this fact.

It might be said with rough truth that all his works were latent in him from his early manhood. Certainly it is true that most of his greater conceptions were nascent in his imagination from the period of his thirties, when he sketched *Die Meistersinger,* completed *Lohengrin,* projected what was eventually to be the vast design of the *Ring,* and when the germs of *Parsifal* (and, a decade later, of *Tristan und Isolde*) were working in the secret depths of his creative will. There is something of each in all, and of all in each.

[4] The first performance of the *Parsifal* score in America was in a concert version by the Oratorio Society of New York under the direction of Walter Damrosch, on March 3, 1886. "It was a good performance," Mr. Damrosch writes me, "and we all, executants as well as the huge audience, were very much moved by the music."

Although it is possible to determine the chronological order in which his works were completed, we do not know how long the substance of any one of his conceptions engaged his mind before he began the long, slow, painful process of shaping its creative form. He was scarcely ever occupied with one conception alone. We find repeatedly that while he seemed to be engrossed with a single absorbing creative task, some other was maturing in his mind and claiming imperiously his attention.[5]

Wagner wrote to August Röckel in the Summer of 1856 that the chief thing he desired was health, "to be able," he said, "to execute all the sketches of which I am full. Unfortunately, I'm fuller than I need: for, beyond the *Nibelungen* pieces [he had finished the scoring of *Die Walküre* a few months earlier], I have still a *Tristan und Isolde* in my head . . . and a latest subject of all, *Die Sieger* [*The Victors*],—supreme redemption, a Buddhist legend. These so compass me about that only with great pertinacity can I drive them back in favor of the *Nibelungen*." He was to begin the music of *Siegfried* a month later. *Die Sieger*[6] was absorbed into

[5] See the extract from Wagner's letter of December 19, 1856, to the Princess Marie Wittgenstein, quoted in the chapter, *Wagner and the Present Day.*

[6] "In *Die Sieger*," he wrote to the Princess Marie Wittgenstein, in March, 1857, "something like this will happen: the maiden

227

Tristan, and (together with elements from the earlier drama, *Jesus of Nazareth*) into *Parsifal.* Is it any wonder that Wagner longed passionately for health in order that he might realize all the life that stirred within him and would not give him peace?

He wrote from Venice to Frau Wesendonck in mid-December, 1858, while he was at work on the mirific Second Act of *Tristan,* and studying philosophy for recreation, that he had "been very busy with *Parsifal.*" [7] Only a fortnight before, he had confided to the diary which he kept for Mathilde: "I could work my whole life long at this [*Tristan*] music. I'm in the Second Act still, but what music it's becoming! . . . O, it grows deep and fair! . . . I have never made a thing like this." Yet *Parsifal*—Kundry, in particular—beckoned him; and he turned aside even from the tyrannous enchantment of *Tristan* to speak with enthusiasm of "an increasingly vital and enthralling conception" which had come to him "of a re-

(Savitri), who, while she waits in Act II for the coming of Ananda, flings herself in transport among the flowers, for very joy absorbing sun, woodland, bird-song, water, all nature into herself, is challenged by Çakya (Buddha), after she had ,made the fateful vow, to look around her and above, and has then to tell what she thinks of it all. 'It is no longer fair,' she says, gravely, sadly; for now she sees the other aspect of the world. . . . In the Second Act of *Tristan*—but you know nothing about that. It is only music as yet . . ."

[7] Incidentally, he was, as he said, "supplementing and correcting my friend Schopenhauer."

228

markable being, a marvellous female world-spirit [ein Weltdämonisches Weib], the messenger of the Grail."

It is a striking instance of his capacity for manifold creative thinking that at one time, when he sketched what appears to have been the earliest draft of the *Tristan* scenario (at Zürich in the latter part of 1854, while he was still composing *Die Walküre*), he intended to bring the pilgrim Parsifal, the black-armored Knight on his weary search for the Holy Grail, to the bedside of the dying Tristan. "On my return from one of my walks," says Wagner in his Autobiography, "I jotted down the incidents of the three Acts [of *Tristan*] in a concise form . . . In the last Act, I introduced an episode, which, however, I did not develop: a visit of Parsifal to Tristan's couch. The vision of the suffering Tristan, wounded but unable to die, identified itself in my mind with Amfortas in the Romance of the Grail."

The plan, of course, was abandoned. Yet *Parsifal* and *Tristan* are inseparably linked, as Wagner well knew, by something more fundamental than that episodic encounter between the two chief characters which he had intended. He let himself go on the subject of *Tristan* versus *Parsifal* in a remarkable letter to Mathilde Wesendonck written from Lucerne on May 30,

1859, while he was agonizing over *Tristan's* final Act.

"I am now at work," he wrote, "on the first half of my Third Act. It always takes me a great deal of time to get through the tragic passages—at best, I can finish very little of these at a sitting. The brisk, swift, fiery parts go much quicker. So, even in the technical working-out, I live it all, 'leidvoll und freudvoll' ['sorrowful and joyful' [8]], and am utterly immersed in my subject. This last Act is a veritable intermittent fever—the deepest, most unutterable suffering and longing, alternating abruptly with inexpressible exultation and jubilation. God knows, no one has ever taken the matter so seriously before, and Semper is quite right.[9] This it is that has set me against *Parsifal* quite recently. Briefly, it has dawned on me again what a truly terrible piece of work this would be. Considered closely, it will be seen that Amfortas is the central point, the main theme . . . Think, in Heaven's name, what it all involves! It has suddenly become terribly clear to me: it is my Tristan of the Third Act inconceivably intensified. With

[8] From Goethe's *Egmont*.

[9] Gottfried Semper was one of a circle of friends to whom Wagner had read the text of *Tristan,* and who, as Wagner records in his Autobiography, "was very angry about it, objecting that I took everything too seriously." Wagner, he tells us, admitted that he would probably get on much more comfortably if he took life more seriously and art more lightly, but that "for the present he meant to let the opposite relations prevail."

the spear-wound, and perhaps another—in his heart—the sufferer, in his terrible anguish, knows only one desire: to die. To win this supreme comfort, he longs for the Vision of the Grail—if only to close the wound; for naught else avails. Yet the Grail, ever and again, gives him but the one boon: that of being *unable* to die; the Vision only multiplies his sufferings by giving them immortality. The Grail, as *I* interpret it, is the Cup of the Last Supper into which Joseph of Arimathea received the Blood of the Saviour upon the Cross. If so, what a fearful significance the relation of Amfortas to this miraculous Cup acquires! Wounded by the spear of a rival in a passionate love adventure, his one hope of healing is in the blessing of that Blood which once flowed from a like wound in the Saviour's side, when, world-renouncing, world-redeeming, world-enduring, He languished upon the Cross. Blood for blood and wound for wound—but what a gulf divides this blood and that, this wound and that! All rapture, all devotion, all ecstasy at the miraculous nearness of the Cup, glowing in its soft and blessed radiance, he draws new life from it—and death cannot come near him! He lives, lives anew, and more terribly than ever the unhallowed wound burns in him— *his* wound. His very devotion becomes a torment. What can end it, where is his salvation? Mortal

231

suffering to all eternity! Divine salvation, guarded by eternal damnation!

"And am I to carry out such a work?—actually make music for it? I thank you! Let him do it who will; *I* shall most politely decline to bow my shoulders to the burden! . . .

"Moreover, Parsifal himself presents another difficulty. He is indispensably necessary as the savior of Amfortas; but if Amfortas is to be set in his true and appropriate light, he becomes of such immense tragic interest that it would be more than difficult to introduce a rival main interest— and yet this must centre in Parsifal if he is not ultimately to appear as a mere, cold, *deus ex machina.* Consequently Parsifal's development, his sublime purification, predestined as it is by everything in his thoughtful, deeply sympathetic nature, must take the foremost place. For this purpose I cannot choose a broad scheme of treatment such as Wolfram had at his disposal. I must compress the whole into three principal dramatic situations of intensive import, in such a way that the theme, at once profound and ramified, shall emerge clearly and distinctly; this way of working, this type of representation, is precisely *my* art. And now—am I to undertake such a task? God forbid! This very day I bid farewell to the mad project."

Happily, his farewell to *Parsifal* was not an everlasting one; for when, in the Summer of 1865, he retreated to a quiet mountain hut on the Hochkopf at the invitation of young King Ludwig, to recover from the shattering blow of Ludwig Schnorr's untimely death after his creation of the role of Tristan at Munich, Wagner, in his mountain solitude, steeped himself in the Hindu poem of the *Ramayana,* and, on his return to Munich, set to work upon the sketch of *Parsifal* desired by the King.

Thenceforth, almost until the end of his life, Wagner held *Parsifal* close to his thoughts. No other of his works sprang from so deep a source in his subconscious mind, nor lived and grew within him for so long a time. For nearly forty years he had dwelt with it, brooded upon its meaning for himself and for his art. Even during the period of his intensest activity, at Bayreuth in the seventies—with the vast and crucial undertaking of the first *Ring* festival to complete—he longed to return to his unfinished work. "I wish all this nonsense were over," he exclaimed, "and that I could get to *Parsifal!*" At Palermo, in 1881-82, the Winter before his death, he worked with feverish haste to complete the instrumentation. On the evening of January 13, 1882, while the Wagner household was celebrating the birthday of their friend Joukowsky, Wagner withdrew to his study. Cosima went to see what he was doing. He was finishing the score of *Parsifal*. "It gave me no peace!" he said. Cosima returned to the birthday party, and soon after, Wagner joined them with the manuscript score in his hand. "On your birthday," he said to Joukowsky, "I have finished my *Parsifal*." Cosima adds the poignant comment: "All the while that he had been working at the score, he had been afraid of being interrupted by death."

Yet, though he was mortally ill, he lived not only to complete the work, but to produce it at Bayreuth in July, 1882, and even to conduct part of the last Act (from the Transformation music to the end) at the final performance of the Festival on August 29th.

As long as it was needed, the steel-like will remained unbroken. But when Wagner and his family went to Venice in the Autumn of 1882 and settled in the Palazzo Vendramini, where he was to end his days, the agonizing spasms of his heart disease increased, and he was haunted by presentiments of death. The last words of his that Cosima recorded in her diary were spoken as he lay in bed the night before he died. They were words of pity and compassion. "I am fond of them," he said, thinking of Alberich and of *Rhein-*

gold "—of the inferior beings of the abyss, of those who are full of longing." [10]

❦ ❦ ❦

It is probable that in *Parsifal* we have the quintessence of Wagner's spiritual and philosophical convictions. The one who knew him best has said of him that he conceived his *Parsifal* "with the rapture and abstraction of a saint and the meditative objectivity of a genius. As in the *Ring* we witness the passing of a myth, the end of a divine world, so, in *Parsifal,* we behold the inception of a religion in its utmost naïveté."

Parsifal is the mystically chosen Agent of the Grail, the instrument of salvation. He is chosen because he is stainless and without guile. Passing unscathed through the most atrocious of temptations, he acquires from that ordeal the enlightenment which desire and its fruit, the agony and grief of men, can bring to the spirit. Through compassion, he becomes mystically and deeply wise. He becomes the Predestined One, the Healer who brings redemption, fulfilling the oracular promise given by the Grail to its sinful guardian, the anguished and repentant Amfortas, as he lay prostrate in prayer before the sanctuary:

[10] He had said, years before, that he was in sympathy with Alberich, "who represents the yearning of the ugly toward that which is beautiful."

"Durch Mitleid wissend,   (Made wise through pity,
Der reine Thor,   The Stainless Fool,
Harre sein',   Wait for him,
Den ich erkor."   My chosen one.)

But Parsifal's deed is subjective. It is not the redemption of Amfortas through the compassion of a guileless simpleton that is the essential fact. The stage of the drama is in the heart of Parsifal himself: it is *his* redemption, *his* regeneration, that is accomplished. There is the vital lesson: that no one may look upon the Grail and know it in the splendid moment of its illumination until he has first become aware of the profound reality of other lives and of the common life—until, in his brother, he has found himself. Wagner would have us realize that this is the true awakening, the true enlightenment: the perception of our common humanity, our common destiny. With that intuition and that knowledge, and not without them, can regeneration be attained. Only thus can we discover our own selves. Only thus can we come closer to immortal things, and know, with a certainty beyond dismay, that, in the Supreme Self, ourselves and all other selves are set, "as the rays are set in the sun."

❦   ❦   ❦

We have already seen that Wagner, as he reflected upon the difficulties of the task that con-

fronted him in the construction of the drama, was
dismayed by the problem of dealing with the character of Parsifal as "a rival main interest" to the
overwhelmingly tragic figure of Amfortas: since
Parsifal, as he realized, "must take the foremost
place." I think he solved that problem—without,
perhaps, quite knowing that he had done so—by
his later realization of the immense potentialities
of Kundry as a factor in the play.

More than a year after he had poured forth
to Mathilde his perplexity over the Parsifal-Am-
fortas problem, he wrote to her again (from
Paris, at the beginning of August, 1860) concerning the troublesome project of his drama of
the Holy Grail. *"Parsifal,"* he said, "has been
stirring in me much again of late. I'm seeing more,
and clearer, in it every day. When it is fully ripe,
the writing of this poem will be an unexampled
joy to me. But many a year may pass before then!
Moreover, I should like to let it rest, for once,
with the poem alone. I'm staving it off as long as
I can, and concern myself with it only when it
takes me by main force. When that happens, this
miraculous power of generation makes me forget
all my misery.

"Didn't I tell you once that the fabulous wild
errand-woman of the Grail is to be one and the
same with the temptress of the Second Act? [See
the reference to Kundry in the passage quoted

earlier in this chapter from Wagner's letter of mid-December, 1858, to Mathilde.] Ever since that dawned on me, almost the whole of this subject has grown clear. This strange, uncanny creature that slave-like serves the Grail-knights with unwearying zeal, fulfills the most untold commissions, and lies cowering in a corner till she's told to execute some office of uncommon hardship, vanishes completely at times, no one knows whither or how. Then suddenly we meet her once again, worn, gruesome, wan, and haggard; yet tireless anew, serving like a hound the Holy Grail. Of its knights, though, she betrays a secret scorn: her eye seems ever seeking for the right one—already has she fancied him, but never found him; nor what she's seeking does she really know: it is sheer instinct. When Parsifal, the dullard, comes into the land, she cannot turn her gaze away from him: some strange thing must be passing in her; she knows it not, but fixes on him. He shudders—but it fascinates him also: nothing does he understand . . .

"This woman is inexpressibly uneasy; the old esquire [Gurnemanz] has remarked it of her oft before, as the time drew near for her to vanish, but her condition this time is at its utmost strain: what is taking place in her? Does she dread another disappearance, from which she longs to be dispensed? Does she hope to be allowed to die at last? What is she hoping of Parsifal? Plainly, she looks to him for something unheard-of—but all is vague and shadowy . . . Huddled in a corner, she is present at Amfortas's scene of agony:[11] sphinx-like, with curious scrutiny, she stares at Parsifal; he, too, is stupid, comprehending nothing, open-mouthed, remaining dumb. He is cast forth: the errand-woman of the Grail sinks shrieking in a heap, then vanishes: she must roam again.

"Now can you guess who is the wondrous, witching woman found by Parsifal in the magic castle whither his knightly temper leads him? Then guess what goes on there, and how it all turns out; for I tell you no more today."

Whether Wagner fully realized the stature to which Kundry grew under his hands as he evolved her in his drama and his music it would be rash to say. But certainly this creation, as it exists in the completed work, is one of the most daring and wonderful in the literature of the stage.

The demoniacal creature of Act I, the wild and hideous servant of the Grail, who becomes in Act II the beautiful temptress of Klingsor's Magic Garden, and finally, in Act III, the sub-

[11] It will be observed that the *Parsifal* drama, as Wagner completed it, departs in several details from this early scheme of Kundry's part in it.

239

dued and humble penitent—this enigmatic character of Wagner's, with her multiplicity of aspects, caused a world of perplexity to early students of *Parsifal*. Kundry has no precise legendary or historic analogue;[12] but we know a little more clearly today, or think we do, what Wagner meant by her. He derived her in part from the character of Prakriti in his Buddhist drama *Die Sieger*—she who was obliged to expiate in her life the sin of pride committed in a prior existence. She is related also to Gundryggia, the wild serving-messenger of Asgard's heroes; to Herodias, doomed by her mockery of Christ on the Cross to wander until she finds once more a savior; and to Mary Magdalen. Kundry is, in short, different incarnations of the same being. She exists "without beginning and without end. She has no individual character, because she is all women at the same time." She is temptress and comforter, courtesan and penitent, queen of lusts and servant of the Grail, destroyer and healer, demon and saint. She has many names, but is nameless. The name changes, the essence remains: that of the multiform Woman, who lives eternally—at once dreadful and alluring, baleful and

[12] In Wolfram's poem, she is only the Grail Messenger; the temptress of the Magic Garden is a beauteous and wholly unrelated character named Orgeluse. Wagner united both in his Kundry.

solacing, ruinous and creative—for the happiness and the agony of men.

Undoubtedly, in Wagner's mind, she personified the tragedy of rebirth, that ancient mystical doctrine of the wanderings of the soul in search of an ultimate resolution and release, with its corollary of external discontent and its unconquerable lust for death. Tristan, Isolde, the Brünnhilde of the Immolation scene, Amfortas, Kundry—each of them has something, much or little, in common with the others: each would understand the others' language.

Wagner must have been fascinated by his creation of Kundry, for he has given her some of his greatest moments of drama and of music. At that passage in the opening scene of the Second Act when she is summoned by Klingsor from the gulf of sleep and time and ceaselessly recurrent death, her dreadful cry as she awakens to the realization of her task has all the anguish of those who may not rest. In the Magic Garden scene, as her voice is heard in that detaining call to Parsifal, the vocal phrase, sustained above an interplay of ninth- and seventh-chords, achieves a ravishing sorcery of sound and evocation. Later, the music that utters her enticements as she weaves her blandishments about the tragically enlightened youth, creates a pattern of allurement that is all loveliness and flowing movement and flame-like grace. And here, too, we are made to realize that Kundry the enchantress, as Wagner's music has enclosed her, is no conventional seductress, but a symbol of immortal longing, a projection of that desirous mind by which men live and die.

Afterward, standing before that redeemer who has come so late, whom, through endless ages, Kundry has awaited, she subdues us by the terrible intensity with which she recalls her mockery of the Saviour on Golgotha. "I saw Him . . . Him," she says, "and—laughed! . . ." A tearing cry of the flutes and piccolo introduces the agonized syllables, *lachte* ("laughed"), with their hysterical descent from the high B to middle C-sharp. Then, after an awe-filled silence, Kundry, accompanied softly in the orchestra by music of immitigable sorrow, tells Parsifal how the suffering, quiet figure on the Cross bent His gaze upon her.[13] The episode, of unspeakable pathos and sublimity, is one to set beside the final moments in the *Crucifixus* of Bach's B minor Mass.

Finally, in that Third Act which is so cruel a test for the interpretative artist (since Wagner has allotted to her only a single word, once re-

[13] Wagner, playing to Cosima this passage—"Ich sah . . . Ihn . . . Ihn . . . und . . . lachte . . . Da traf mich . . . sein Blick" ("I saw . . . Him . . . Him . . . and . . . laughed . . . His glance fell on me"), said to her that he was curious to know if she "would recognize the glance." She said, "It is that of Dürer's Christ at Nuremberg, is it not?" and he answered that it was.

peated), Kundry, in the rough garb of a penitent, stands motionless for long moments during the recitals and colloquies of Parsifal and Gurnemanz, grave and sad and inarticulate, looking backward through the ages and her many pasts. She makes no gesture, no change of pose, she scarcely moves her head; yet in the pose itself, in the vision within the eyes, in the contour and plane and pallor of the profile, she gives us a poignant sense of that recurrent moment in which the spirit pauses in its pilgrimage beyond the path of time, embodying the immemorial tragedy and grief and loneliness of this woman of uncounted incarnations, the symbol of Nature and of life itself.

The blend of visual and aural impressiveness in *Parsifal* is one of the distinguishing traits of the work. We know from Wagner's own observations how important a part the visual image played in the fertilization of his musical imagination, and how important, from his own point of view, was the blending of the two. His mind, as Monsieur Charles Tardieu long ago observed in a searching comment upon *Parsifal,* was evidently filled with repercussions of the religious paintings of the early German, Flemish, and Italian masters; and he has fused these wonderfully with his music. The effect, when the various elements are sensitively realized and combined, is unforgettable. It is especially so in the Good Friday

243

scene. Gurnemanz blesses Parsifal, the deliverer of Amfortas, and Parsifal, in turn, seated beside the holy spring, baptizes Kundry, who anoints his feet and dries them with her long hair, "like a Magdalene by Mabuse—for the musician takes upon his palette of sound the tones that the painter would have drawn from his color-box"; and the suggestion of the central panel from some inconceivably moving triptych becomes complete and overwhelming. This expressiveness is deepened by the tragedy of Kundry's weeping when she bends before the pitying gentleness of the enlightened Parsifal as he gazes on the peacefulness of the blossoming Spring meadows, while the tenderness of the oboe's song of penitence and pardon, and the murmuring of the muted strings, surround like an aureole of sound the rapt and motionless figures and make them part of the miracle that they evoke.

❦   ❦   ❦

But the heart of *Parsifal* is, as always with Wagner, in the music; and this music is in some respects the most wonderful that he has left us.

It is sometimes said (usually by those who are impatient with the nonmusical aspects of the work—its drama, ethics, philosophy) that in this score Wagner's power of invention was on the wane. This opinion is not shared by those who

best know the score, and who are mindful of the
qualities that distinguish the music of *Tristan,
Die Meistersinger,* and the *Ring.* Wagner's invention was never more subtle, choice, and resourceful than it is in *Parsifal.* Not every page of it is
upon the same transcendent level—as not every
moment of the B minor Mass or the Ninth Symphony is equally to be treasured. It is possible to
feel that in certain measures of *Parsifal* (for example, in the E-flat section of the chorus in Act
I beginning at "Wein und Brot des letzten Mah-
les") Wagner's power of self-scrutiny suffered
a minor lapse. But what countless prodigies of
beauty, what piercing expressiveness, this music
of *Parsifal* contains! For the most part, the score
proceeds upon the highest plane of inspiration,
with one of its twin peaks at the beginning of the
Good Friday scene, where the Parsifal and Grail
themes are magnified in their B major apotheosis
(a feat worthy of the musical imagination that
transformed Siegfried's horn call into the stupendous funeral hymn of the Dirge in *Götterdämmerung*), and its other peak shining with
pentecostal radiance in the transfiguration of the
Faith theme at the end of the drama—the scene of
the Glorification, with the indescribable entrance
of the voices at "Höchsten Heiles Wunder!"

The prevailingly slow pulse of the music, the

245

hieratic grandeur and solemnity that fill so many pages of the score, are implicit in its character. The exhibition of the rich and glowing fabrics of Wagner's orchestra, their fold upon fold of intricate, subdued magnificence, is not to be accomplished on the run, or by a turn of the wrist. They accumulate splendor; and we think of the slow, superb crescendo of Jehovah's prescription for Aaron's priestly robes—"gold, and blue, and purple, and scarlet, . . . and fine twined linen; . . . sardius, and topaz, and emerald, and sapphire, and diamond; agate, amethyst, beryl, and jasper." Yet there are many times when the music is not magnificent, moments filled with that mystical poignancy which is this music's inner voice. There are other moments, still more wonderful, when it has that quality which Wagner said that he wanted to achieve in his instrumentation of the work—"the character of cloud-formations, which separate and then unite again," when the music seems to yield some disembodied loveliness of sound that hovers above the players and the instruments, and we become aware of beatific presences and otherworldly lights. And, as the curtains fall, we are one with the worshipping company prostrate before the cumulative revelation of immortal beauty.

❀   ❀   ❀

Parsifal has been fortunate in most of the interpreters who have set the work before that portion of the American public which has known it longest and best—those listeners who attend the yearly performances at the Metropolitan Opera House. *Parsifal* is the one great work in the repertoire of the operatic theatre of today whose appeal cannot survive a performance unquickened by insight and affection, and unexalted by imaginative faith. Its moods and its style are not to be comprehended or conveyed by the casual or the unelect. The ablest interpreters of the work at the Metropolitan in recent years have left us in no doubt of the fact that they had been caught up into the work's essential moods. Lauritz Melchior's Parsifal has been his capital achievement. He has grown extraordinarily in his mastery of its musical style since he first sang it at Bayreuth a decade or so ago. One has not heard him do anything more just and telling, in this or in another role, than his delivery of the compassionate and exquisite phrases in which he addresses Kundry in the Good Friday scene after she has anointed his feet and dried them with her unbound hair; and again, as he baptizes her; and lastly, as he shows her the sweet tranquillity of the Spring woods and the meadows gleaming in the morning light.

Those moods, those accents, are not easily

captured. The music here is of penetrating subtlety and tenderness and exaltation, of a quality
that can easily be nullified by the slightest touch
of crudity or false emotion. Mr. Melchior summons the necessary mood with a delicacy and
rightness beyond praise. One will not soon forget
the tone and phrasing and enunciation of his ". . .
an den Erlöser," and, after, of "du weinest, . . .
sieh, es lacht die Aue!"

As for Mme. Flagstad, the quality of her
Kundry was made known to us when she assumed
the baffling part at the Metropolitan in 1935 for
the first time in her career. Her roles are being
constantly enriched in beauty and significance
from the seemingly inexhaustible store of her inspired sympathy and comprehension; and her
Kundry shares in that process.

The music of the role had never been sung
here as she sings it, nor the words of the text
enunciated with the fullness of meaning which
she gives them. The two syllables, once repeated,
that are the whole of her part in the Third Act,
are required by Wagner to bear a weight and a
power of extension demanding almost the impossible of Kundry's impersonator; yet as Mme.
Flagstad utters them, they epitomize what had
gone before in this drama of spiritual conquest
through submission, and imply what is to follow
in the consummation of Wagner's luminous

parable of renunciatory love. The pantomime whereby she throws fresh lights and saliencies upon its meaning has seemed more telling with every performance: the desperate tragedy of the garden duologue, the eloquence of her tense in-action in the penitential scene, when Kundry lives for us that moment in which time becomes eternity—these things have been given for us a new dimension and significance.

❦   ❦   ❦

It should be said, for the possible information of posterity, that to many now living, no conductor has in our time conveyed the essentials of the music of *Parsifal,* in the American concert-room and at Bayreuth, with the depth and fineness of comprehension, the priestly elevation, the purity of style, that Arturo Toscanini imparts to it. Listening to this music as he releases it, one seems to be aware of some constituent of light that has become sound, of aspiration that has become beauty. For many, it has been a matchless experience to hear this music as he releases it— chiefly because *Parsifal* is the ultimate Wagner, and because Wagner is what he is; but also because Toscanini is what he is, and because his conducting of the music of *Parsifal* crowns his life's achievements.

For him, no art that is great art, whether or

not it be "religious" in the narrower and limiting sense of the word, has ever or could ever move from the temple. Yet the completeness with which *Parsifal* illustrates Wagner's conception of the true function of the theatre seems to have made inevitable its confrontation by Toscanini. He is doubtless its predestined custodian. His raptness in his chosen task; his attitude of consecration; his utter self-effacement; the image that he summons of the priest before the altar: these things mark him out for *Parsifal* and *Parsifal* for him.

As he transmits the music, there are subtleties within subtleties, an infinite sensibility in the tracing of line and the application of harmonic and instrumental color, a saturation of the musical idea in beauty of a transilluminated purity— to recall a few among innumerable instances, the enunciation of the altered theme of Faith as it threads the singer's words in the latter part of Gurnemanz's narrative; and the slow unfolding of the A-flat passage for the strings which accompanies Kundry's visit to the spring with her pitcher, and her announcement of Parsifal's approach. His slow tempi are slower even than Muck's, but their rectitude is beyond dispute. The pace of the music seems inevitable and preordained, and it is often overpowering in effect—as in the episode of Parsifal's adoration of the sacred Spear.

His reading has not only breadth and depth and loftiness of mood, and that mystical intensity without which the music of *Parsifal* does not live, but it is also sharply and startlingly dramatic. The tautness and incisiveness and vitality of the rhythms in such passages as the first entrance of Kundry and the stormy introduction of the Second Act, are scarcely less remarkable than the probing agony with which Toscanini charges certain of those lacerating measures in which the music seems to bear the cumulative burden of humanity's immemorial woe, transfixing the spirit with its pity and its grief—when one feels as if it had remembered Hamlet's plea, and drew its breath in pain.

❧ ❧ ❧

Wagner's *Parsifal* is rife with marvels; but perhaps the greatest of these is the sense of mysterious and profound assuagement with which the music at its noblest is filled, as if the old master in the evening of his tempestuous life had wanted to show us, as he unveiled for the last time this glowing chalice of his miraculous art, that the innermost secret of all beauty is its benison of profound appeasement.

His final masterpiece reveals with unexampled clarity the source from which his greatest music sprang, the music of certain transcendental pages in *Tristan* and in *Parsifal:* pages in which we find a stainless image of that central peace, existing at the heart of endless agitation, which Wordsworth knew. Wagner, like Wordsworth and like Beethoven, could find his way to that region of mystical reverie and contemplation, "in which self itself evaporates, and consciousness floats free, intense and luminous and serene."

Epilogue

THOSE of us who listen today to Wagner's operas, more than half a century after his death, may perhaps be reminded of what a wise and inspired poet has said about the signs that tell us how we may know a master. Among those signs, he said, are the artist's manifest delight in life's abundance, and a sense of the depth and vastness of its mystery. The lonely group of music's towering creators have let us share that god-like savoring of the whole of life, and that sense of its mystery which is beyond our reach. But in Wagner, one is inclined to think, those qualities are excelling; for in all the music that bespeaks him truly, the life that it proclaims is the life of ecstasy, the life of "high states of the soul, great loves, generosities, endeavors, and great downfalls and endurances, and a mighty flowing-in of light."

Everywhere in Wagner's greater works is this artist's blend of grandeur and exquisiteness, his cutting of cameos and his twining of golden threads, and the mountain chains that his imagination throws against the sky. Always his speech is level with his imagination, his vision, his sympathies, his will. He is the master of a language so manifold, so magical, that it can say the final thing about a linden's fragrance and a god's defeat, and light the far horizons of the spirit's world.

Other makers of great music have been at home in regions to which he was a stranger, or have entered doors for which he had no key. But in no house of the singing spirit are there so many mansions as in his; in no other habitation of the musical mind are there so many beautiful and living presences; so many windows, open to so many enthralling visions of the world.

Perhaps it is not possible, as we have been reminded, to speak of poetry or of music or of those other immortal energies of mortal man without submission to something not understood, something that is greater than the perishing self. But we may know in what presence we are standing if we bear in mind that the language of the gods is such that it survives forever in the ears and hearts of men, "triumphant over Death and Time." It is true that Time is full of lost and wandering airs that once had fame and habitation. Yet some will continue to cherish that bravest of delusions: that there is, after all, a deathless beauty. Listening to music such as Wagner's, we believe again, and we are taught once more what it will always mean to stand beside a dead

254

man's marvels, and (as Chesterton said of his St. Francis) have nothing to offer in response but some brief candle burnt out so quickly before his shrine.

APPENDIX

A Note on Wagner's Motives

WAGNER'S operas, now preëminent in the repertoires of the Metropolitan and other lyric theatres of America, attract increasingly the interest of a new generation of music lovers and students, who, thanks in large measure to the stimulating influence of the gramophone [1] and the radio, wish to hear stage performances of the works themselves. Doubtless many of these actual and potential Wagnerians, just beginning their acquaintance with the *Ring* or *Tristan* or *Die Meistersinger* or *Parsifal,* are asking, as their elders did before them, "Is it necessary to know the 'motives,' and, if so, what is the best way to learn them?"

The first part of that question revives an old subject of dispute, one that seems to be in perpetual need of clarification. As to the second part of the question, there are, surprisingly enough, some new things to be said, for the reason that a new factor has lately entered the case.

---

[1] The student is referred, if he does not already know it, to *The Gramophone Shop Encyclopedia of Recorded Music,* the monumental reference work compiled by R. D. Darrell and published in 1936 by the Gramophone Shop, Inc., New York. In this indispensable guide no fewer than twenty-seven pages are devoted to annotated lists of the recorded repertoire of Wagner's music.

APPENDIX

In the early days of the reign of Richard the First, Wagnerian neophytes were often told that they could not hope to enjoy performances of the later music-dramas unless they were able to affix a label to every one of the leading-motives in the scores. The late William Ashton Ellis, in his uncompleted Life of Wagner, drew an amusing picture of a group of Wagnerian innocents preparing for a Bayreuth festival: "earnest souls whom a more experienced friend was coaching, so that they could remember the labels of certain groups of sounds! After a few preliminary lessons the victims would be put through their paces: a motive was struck on the piano, and they were expected to fish up its orthodox name from their overcrowded memories. The natural result was that most of their time in the Bayreuth theatre was spent in a desperate endeavor to translate into terms of the piano (their vehicle of instruction) the orchestral combinations that they were hearing for the first time. Even if the motives were always named with approximate logic and consistency, what pleasure could be left for those students who had bemused themselves with details long before they knew the whole?"

Many other commentators, annoyed by the trustfulness with which Wagnerian beginners are inclined to assume that a memorizing of Lavignac's or Wolzogen's titled quotations of the motives is an adequate substitute for a thoroughgoing study of Wagner's text and music, have asserted in their irritation that a knowledge of the significance of the themes is unnecessary. "If Wagner's music vitalizes the drama for you," declares a well-known writer, "it matters not whether you know the motives."

To say that, is to darken counsel. It matters enormously "whether you know the motives"—it matters so much, indeed, that many passages in Wagner's music-dramas are deprived of their dramatic or poetical significance for those who do not know the meaning of the themes from which they are evolved.

It is possible, of course, for the uninstructed hearer to listen to one of Wagner's scores merely as a tissue of instrumental and vocal sound, and to derive intense aesthetic pleasure from the ceaseless glow and richness of the musical fabric. It is also possible, if one knows the drama and is familiar with the text, to be stirred and held by the incomparable eloquence of the music as an enhancing expression of the action and the words. It is unquestionably true that Wagner's music is not only beautiful and engrossing simply as music, but that it does (in the words of the commentator I have quoted) ceaselessly "vitalize the drama," even if one does not "know the motives."

But it is a grave error to suppose that *Die Walküre* or *Götterdämmerung* or *Tristan* can be understood or appreciated—or, indeed, enjoyed to the full—by those who are unaware of the significance of those uniquely expressive "leading-motives," or "guiding-themes," wherewith Wagner spins his marvellous symphonic web—that ceaselessly revealing and enlightening commentary which was a new thing under the sun [2] when Wagner disclosed it to the world.

Far from being mere names or labels for objects and abstractions, or tonal "visiting-cards" for the characters,—as Debussy stupidly alleged,—Wagner's motives, as he pointed out in his *Zukunftsmusik* essay, perform a function akin to that of the Greek chorus, interpreting, revealing, remembering, foretelling, elucidating, conveying a depth and pregnancy of meaning or association that words alone would be powerless to suggest. "In the total expression," says Wagner in his *Opera and Drama,* "the orchestra takes an unbroken share, supporting and elucidating on every hand: it is the moving matrix of the music . . . The chorus of Greek tragedy has bequeathed to us its significance for the drama in the modern orchestra, and therein, free from any hampering, has evolved to an immeasurable wealth of utterance."

❦ ❦ ❦

Let us imagine an uninstructed Wagnerian hearing *Die Walküre* for the first time. At that point in Siegmund's narrative where he tells of having sought in vain the father whom he knew as "Wolfe," our uninstructed listener would hear in the orchestra a strikingly noble and majestic phrase in E major played softly by the trombones. Doubtless he would think the

---

[2] Leading-motives had been used in dramatic music long before Wagner's time; but no one had ever employed them with the consistency, elaboration, and expressiveness that they achieve in Wagner's later works.

passage very beautiful; but it could not possibly yield him the associative richness and the imaginative stir that it yields to us, who are aware that we are hearing the Valhalla theme, and that the orchestra is telling us what Siegmund himself does not know: that his father "Wolfe" was really Wotan.

This is an obvious example of the almost unlimited power of dramatic and poetical illumination, explication, and intensification which Wagner is enabled to exert through his use of guiding-themes. Let us take another example, somewhat less obvious: As Isolde, in Act I of *Tristan*, signs to Brangäne to bring the Death-Potion that she intends for Tristan, the latter, roused from his dark brooding by the shouts of the crew reducing sail, cries out, "Where are we?" Isolde's answer, "Near the goal!" has a double meaning rich in tragic irony; but that double meaning will escape us unless we are aware that the motive accompanying her words is the motive of Death.[3]

In Act III of *Tristan*, the arrival of Isolde's ship is announced by the jubilant tune played off-stage by the watching shepherd. Tristan, frantic with joy, dispatches Kurvenal to the shore to aid Isolde, and, his frenzy redoubled, tosses in unbearable impatience upon his couch. He tears the bandage from his wound, rises to his feet, and staggers toward the approaching Isolde, who, entering breathlessly, receives her dying lover in her arms as the orchestra voices their emotions in one

[3] In the Corder translation, used in certain scores and librettos, Isolde's answer, "Hart am Ziel," is rendered, "Near to shore," which quite obliterates Isolde's double meaning.

of the unendurable moments of the marvellous score. This outburst of tragic passion, beautiful and despairing, overwhelms the spirit, at the same time that it fills with wondering admiration the appreciative mind of the musician: for the passage is a miracle of contrapuntal art. Yet the effect upon the listener is immeasurably enhanced if, bearing in mind the preceding phases of the drama, he is aware that the instrumental fabric at this point is woven of no fewer than half a dozen motives, each one contributing its piercingly reminiscent allusion to some mood or scene or incident that has gone before: the motive of the signalling Torch, the motive of Death, a theme from the love duo of Act II, a phrase from the orchestral nocturne that accompanied Brangäne's song of warning, and the motives of Sorrow and of Desire [4] first heard at the beginning of the Prelude to the opera.

Yet again, consider that moment in Siegfried's *Götterdämmerung* narrative when he pauses after telling the assembled hunters how he killed the treacherous Mime. Hagen knows that Siegfried remembers nothing of what followed—his first ascent of the flaming mountain and his winning of Brünnhilde: for the potion given him by Gutrune has erased those memories from his mind. So now, as Siegfried halts his recital, Hagen, who wishes him to complete the story that he has to tell, presses upon him a draught that will restore the hero's memory. As Siegfried drains the potion and resumes his tale, we hear from the 'cellos a cantilena of melancholy beauty. No lover of Wagner—no lover of

---

[4] Sometimes called the motive of Isolde's Magic.

musical loveliness, indeed—could resist the beauty of this passage; but only the instructed Wagnerian, aware that the theme sung by the 'cellos is the motive of Brünnhilde, can feel to the end of this moment's poignancy, as Siegfried's memories of all his hours with Brünnhilde begin to throng into his mind, while the falling dusk gathers about the predestined figure on the stage and seems to descend upon the instruments, clothing with ineffable sadness the haunted beauty of the music.

Wagner might almost have been anticipating the effect of this kind of integrating thematic allusion when he said, in a striking passage from his *Communication to My Friends* (written in 1851) : "Just as, in the progress of the drama, the intended climax of a chief and decisive mood was to be reached only through a development, continuously present to the feeling, of the individual moods already aroused, so must the musical expression . . . necessarily take a decisive share in this development to a climax. This has been brought about, quite of itself, in the form of a characteristic tissue of principal themes, that spreads itself not over one scene only . . . but over the whole drama, in intimate connection with the poetic aim."

Such commentaries as these are scattered innumerably through Wagner's scores, ranging the gamut from direct allusion to the subtlest suggestiveness. And this is the wonderful and complex vehicle of interpretation which certain impatient critics would have us disregard! "Enjoy the music without bothering about the motives," wrote one of them. Well, we may follow that course if we choose. It is the easier way. The point to decide for one's self, after all, is what one expects to get out of such a work as *Tristan* or the *Ring*. We may react to it passively, receptively, deriving what we can from it without bestirring ourselves much in the process. Or, we may react to it coöperatively, ardently, responsively, and thus find ourselves surprisingly enriched.

        ❦   ❦   ❦

I have, perhaps, suggested the basis for a reasonable answer to the first part of the question that I supposed the Wagnerian beginner might ask: "Is it necessary to know the motives?" The answer to the question's second part—"What is the best way to learn them?"—had best be prefaced by the warning that no study of the music of any one of Wagner's works should ever be undertaken without a thorough knowledge of the dramas. The beginner, if he is wise, will master, first, the text, the plays themselves. Without knowing thoroughly the words of every one of the forty-odd scenes that comprise the *Ring,* for example, one cannot hope to understand the music. Know the words: that is the cardinal principle.

As for the best way to learn the motives, we should remind ourselves that we must not be too rigidly schematic in attaching names to these guiding-themes. There is a certain class of motive that, as Ernest Newman has pointed out, seems to have been associated in Wagner's mind with generalized moods rather than with concrete and definite conceptions that can be fixed in a single word. Certain themes appear to mean different things at this point or other of the dramas in which they appear.

Furthermore, it should be remembered that Wagner was not responsible for the labels that have become attached to his themes. Those of the *Ring* were, apparently, first named by a German-American, Gottlieb Federlein, who in 1871-72 (five years before the production of the *Ring* as a whole) sent from America to a German paper a serial analysis of the *Rheingold* and *Walküre* scores. Wolzogen took over and continued Federlein's labors; and after Wolzogen came the deluge.

There is more than one unsolved problem contained in the music of Wagner's scores. The identifying of certain motives is not always easy; and the commentators do not invariably help us. They are sometimes in disagreement not only concerning the names of the motives, but concerning their significance. For example, the famous passage of chromatically descending chords that is heard in the Finale of *Die Walküre* as Wotan announces to Brünnhilde his decree that she must lie bound in sleep, has various names, depending upon the commentator whom you happen to be reading —it is the motive of "Departing Godhood," of "Twilight," of "Eternal Sleep," of "Erda the Earthmother," of "The Magic Ban." On the other hand, certain of the more familiar appellations, those upon which most of the commentators are agreed, are under suspicion— as, for instance, the so-called "Flight" motive from the *Ring,* first heard in *Das Rheingold.*

APPENDIX

There are mysterious and eluding things in the *Ring,* as there are in all extensive and full-stored works of the imagination. But most of the motives in the gigantic opus are reasonably self-explanatory; and the soundest advice that a veteran Wagnerian can offer is that the student had best work out for himself the problem of the motives' associations with the drama, basing his study on a scrutiny of the words and of the scores themselves. The guidebooks will help, if it is borne in mind that they are, like fire, excellent servants but dangerous masters.

❦   ❦   ❦

At the commencement of these remarks I referred to the fact that there are some new things to be said concerning the best way to learn certain of the motives for the reason that a new factor has of late entered into the problem. This new factor is the gramophone, that has suddenly and unexpectedly proved itself to be an almost ideal assistant to the Wagnerian beginner who wishes to familiarize himself with the musical characteristics of the principal themes in the *Ring.* For half a century, students have wrestled with piano reductions of the Wagner scores (some of them distortingly simplified, some of them formidably difficult) in an effort to absorb their thematic contents. It is still necessary, of course, to know the scores in their entirety; and to this end the student who cannot read the orchestral originals must perforce rely upon piano transcriptions. But for the purpose of studying the motives, the scores and the guidebooks may now be supplemented, in the case of the *Ring,* by a novel and invaluable aid: a phonographic reproduction of the chief themes in their orchestral form, with references by an announcer to a printed list of titles. Why this simple and inspired method has not been put in practice before, I have no idea. But let us rejoice that we can benefit by it now.

At the headquarters of those enterprising and enlightened friends of music, the specialists in gramophone records, you can procure, for a modest sum, a set of H.M.V.-Victor records, comprised on four sides of two twelve-inch discs, that will play for you ninety motives from *Der Ring des Nibelungen.* The recording was made by the London Symphony Orchestra, under the direction of Lawrance Collingwood.

This is the way the method works: The first record starts off with the initial motive of *Das Rheingold.* You refer to the printed list that accompanies the records, giving each motive in musical notation, with its number and title. From this you learn that Motive No. 1 is that which the H.M.V. analysts call "Nature." There is a brief pause, and a very English voice, speaking from the record, says "Two!" whereupon the invisible orchestra plays the second motive. This is, as you learn from the printed list, entitled "The Waves." And so on, through the rest of the chosen ninety (several important motives, as those of Fate and Hagen, are, unfortunately, omitted). In each case, the very English voice announces the number of the motive to be played, and the printed list makes everything plain.

The names of the motives are derived by the

gramophone company from unavowed authorities. Not everyone will agree with their fitness; but all such names, as I have said, are in some degree open to question; and these, in the main, serve their purpose.

The motives are effectively exhibited by the orchestra; and it is an invaluable aid to the student to be able to hear them in their characteristic instrumental colors, instead of being obliged to study them in monochromatic approximations on a piano keyboard. Thus do the maligned substitutions of the Machine Age turn out, ironically, to be the means of bringing us nearer to ideal things.